D0175137

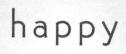

happy

ALSO BY IAN K. SMITH, M.D.

The 4 Day Diet

Extreme Fat Smash Diet

The Fat Smash Diet

The Take-Control Diet

Dr. Ian Smith's Guide to Medical Websites

The Blackbird Papers: A Novel

happy

Simple Steps to Get the Most Out of Life

Ian K. Smith, M.D.

ST. MARTIN'S PRESS

NEW YORK

The names and identifying characteristics of some persons described in this book have been changed.

www.stmartins.com

Book design by Ellen Cipriano

LIBRARY OF CONGRESS CATALOGING-IN-PUBLICATION DATA

Smith, Ian, 1969–
  Happy : simple steps to get the most out of life / Ian K. Smith. —1st ed.
    p. cm.
  ISBN 978-0-312-60635-0 *4342* *1030* *05/10*
  1. Happiness.   2. Conduct of life.   I. Title.
BJ1481.S593 2010
170—dc22   2010002169

First Edition: May 2010

10 9 8 7 6 5 4 3 2 1

To Tristé, Dashiell, and Declan.
No mere mortal has ever been so blessed.
My supreme happiness is waking up every day knowing
that you exist and that we are one.

contents

Introduction

The Epiphany

✧

Gratitude bestows reverence, allowing us to encounter everyday epiphanies, those transcendent moments of awe that change forever how we experience life and the world.

—JOHN MILTON

For me it happened on the other side of the world in a small resort on the South China Sea. I was into the third day of my honeymoon on this remote tropical island, and my body was finally starting to relax. Life didn't get better than this. I had just wed the love of my life, and now we were spending a week together away from our demanding jobs and hectic lives. We had even reached an agreement during the twenty-hour flight on the issue of my compulsion to be "connected." I agreed to connect to the Internet only twice a day—first thing in the morning when we got up, and sometime at night before we fell asleep. I had a lot going on at work at the time, so the thought of having no communication with the rest of the world for a whole week—my bride's first proposal—was a non-starter for me. But two 30-minute sessions per day was an arrangement I could handle.

The morning session wasn't a problem. I have always been a morning person, typically waking early even on weekends when I can focus without the phone ringing or my Black-Berry exploding. My plan was simple: I would get up while my wife was still asleep and take the ten-minute walk to the main lodge. Wireless Internet connections were not available in our individual villas but only inside the guest reception cabin. I couldn't help but think that this restricted access had been intentionally designed by the resort managers—their gentle reminders that we were on vacation.

The walk was refreshing, with the cooler morning temperatures a lot more bearable than the oppressive humidity that fell on us later in the afternoon. While the resort slept, the animals played, swinging overhead in the trees or scurrying across the cart path that meandered through the pristine property. With the fog burning off the sea's calm waters and the rising sun climbing above the horizon, everything was postcard perfect. The main lodge area was always cooled by the purring air conditioners, and the attentive staff was already busy at work preparing for another day of impeccable service to its international guests. I connected to the Internet via my laptop, read some of the national news sites, and then finished what remained of my half hour by reading and answering e-mails. By the time I got back to our villa, my wife was waking, and we went for a long walk on the deserted beach before breakfast.

My evening session proved a little trickier, however. Because of the time difference it made sense for me to wait until 11 p.m. or midnight for my Internet-fix. This gave me the best opportunity to communicate with people in the States when they would be at work and sitting in front of their computers. The difficulty was that while the grounds of the resort were picturesque and great to walk through in the daylight, they were extremely dark at night, making the scurrying critters and howling animals a bit unnerving. The resort offered a twenty-four-hour shuttle service for its guests. All we had to do was dial a number, and within minutes a golf cart appeared outside the villa, manned by a driver always offering a smile and a bottle of chilled water regardless of the hour. The resort thought of everything.

I typically called around midnight, long after the main lodge had been closed and locked, the staff having returned to their cramped bunks to squeeze out a few hours of sleep. As I got into the cart one night, I looked at my driver, a slight man in his late twenties, simply dressed, his smile not able to completely hide the fatigue in the corners of his eyes. It was obvious that I had woken him up, but he remained extremely cheerful and helpful, without betraying even the smallest hint of annoyance at my untimely interruption. I usually took the short ride to the lodge in silence, but that night curiosity got the best of me.

"Do you use the Internet?" I asked.

"No," he said with a smile. "I don't use the computer. But you like the computer, no?"

"I guess you could say that," I replied. "It's the best way to keep track of what's happening back at home and at work."

"Work? You worry about work while on vacation?"

He asked it innocently and wisely, and delicately enough to get his point across without offending. That one question from a stranger cut to the heart of what I already knew but refused to see.

"I'm on vacation, but the world keeps spinning," I said, immediately feeling like some overcharged type-A urbanite, an intruder in this peaceful and simple rural Indonesian society.

We rode a little farther, listening to unseen animals calling to one another in the smoldering darkness.

"Have you ever been to New York City?" I asked.

"Never." He smiled.

"Don't you want to see the greatest city in the world?"

"Of course," he replied. He hit the brakes as a small ball of dark fur ran in front of the cart and then disappeared into the wooded hillside.

"So when are you going?" I asked.

"I'm not," he said matter of factly.

"Why?"

"I could never afford it," he said. "Too much money."

"But you could save for it and then go," I said. "At least once. You'd love it. It's amazing to see all the people and the lights and buildings. Nothing like here. You would never forget it."

He shook his head. "I hear about New York City all the time," he said. "I see the pictures in the magazine. But I never save enough money to go. How much would I pay to fly?"

"Maybe seventeen hundred dollars," I said.

He shrugged. "Never," he said quietly.

We rode in silence up the steep hill, the cart's engine straining as we climbed.

"If you don't mind my asking, how much money do you earn each month?" I asked.

"We do better here at the resort than others," he said. "We work long days, but we make good money. About 2.4 million rupiah."

I did the calculation in my head. "That's two hundred U.S. dollars," I said, "per month?"

"Good money for us." He nodded.

"You can live on two hundred dollars?" I asked.

"Easy," he said, rolling the car quietly over the winding pavement. The angled roof of the lodge was just coming into view.

"How do you pay for everything with such little money?"

"I have all that I need," he said. "It's enough for me and my family."

"And you're happy with that?"

"Very happy." He nodded. "We are happy people here. We're thankful for what we have, and we enjoy it." Then he looked at me and smiled. "You can't miss what you don't have."

I was numb. Here I was on the other side of the world in the middle of the night on my honeymoon, scrambling to get an Internet connection so that I could work and keep up with everything I thought was important, and a man in a simple uniform, with sleep clinging to the corners of his eyes and making $200 a month, had just held up a mirror to my soul. What I saw tore a whole in my stomach.

We arrived at the lodge, and he got out to unlock the door for me.

"Is there anything else I can get you?" he asked.

"I'm good," I said. "Thanks for the ride and the conversation."

"What time would you like me to pick you up?" he asked.

"I won't need a ride," I said, shaking my head. "Tonight I'll walk back."

He bowed his head, got into his cart, and drove off to the staff cabin that I later learned housed more than twenty men in a space that wasn't much bigger than my apartment in New York City.

I didn't fall asleep easily that night. I kept thinking about my life back in New York, as a physician and journalist, the chaos and stress and angst I fought through on a daily basis. And it wasn't just me. Millions of us were trapped in this concrete jungle, racing and competing the second we stepped outside our tiny apartments. The images of my life kept flashing like a movie stuck in a loop: fighting for cabs during the morning rush hour, long lines of people standing at bus stops, mothers struggling to fold a stroller with one hand while holding their baby with the other as they stuffed themselves into the back of taxis.

What kind of life was I leading? Why was I putting myself through such stress? Even with all that I had, was the expensive shirt from Façonnable on Fifth Avenue or the annual bump in my salary worth the endless hassle? Did these things *really* make me happier? Disappointment choked me as I realized that I had lost my bearings and gotten swept away in a world of me-first materialism, a world that defined success and happiness by the number of zeroes at the end of bank account balances, the square footage of apartments, and the ability to whip around Manhattan by private car service.

I started to feel like Charlie Sheen in the movie *Wall Street*, someone who wanted success so badly that he sold his soul to the devil of greed to get it. What made it hurt even more is that I certainly hadn't been born into a world of luxurious excess. I had grown up in a simple community in a small out-of-the-way town in Connecticut where you could leave the house key under the front mat and let your car run at the gas pump when you went inside to pick up a can of soda. Our parents and grandparents didn't sit around the dinner table strategizing about ways to get us accepted into exclusive private schools or renting beach houses in the Hamptons. They worked hard for their modest possessions, and they were proud of them. We didn't have everything, but we made do—happily—with what we had. Gratitude was nonnegotiable. It was mandatory that we get down on our knees every night and thank God for what He provided.

For the rest of my honeymoon, that conversation with the golf cart driver wouldn't leave me alone. It was the first time in a long time that I really *thought* about the meaning of happiness and whether it applied to my life. If you had asked all my family, friends, and coworkers whether I was a happy person, the unanimous answer would be yes. Some would mention how hard I worked and how busy I always seemed to be, but they would agree that I was a happy person. But now I was second-guessing what I had taken as an absolute truth for so long. What was it that was making me happy? As we waited for dinner to be served, I jotted down on the back of my napkin the first things that came to mind:

Wife

Family

Friends

Job

Future financial security

Car

Living in New York City

Graduating from great schools

Reading a good book

What happened to me that night in that golf cart as I rode along the dark China Sea was an epiphany. I didn't know it at the time, but it would change forever how I would experience life and the world. I now understood how a friend of mine who had gone to Brown University and was making millions during Wall Street's heyday could suddenly give it up and report over a lazy Saturday brunch that he was going into the ministry. *The ministry?* The rest of us—all men, all deeply invested in the idea that it was our destiny to become the next class of New York City titans—seriously thought our friend was either suffering from a career-ending drug habit none of us knew anything about or had been diagnosed with a terminal illness and decided to spend the last of his days seeking spiritual redemption. It never occurred to us that maybe he was making this change simply because he genuinely wanted to pursue a passion that had nothing to do with money or social standing.

There was nothing wrong with Chris. He was healthy, and despite the pleas of his bosses to stay with the firm, he turned down the millions more they offered him and stuck with his decision. He told me privately that he had had fun on Wall Street and certainly made an incredible living, but there was so much more he wanted to do with his life, so much more he wanted to give to others so that they might have some of the opportunities he had been fortunate enough to experience. The prestigious job and all the creature comforts it afforded were not making him happy. While sitting at his desk in the middle of a busy trading day, he had had his epiphany. Looking at his screen full of trades worth billions of dollars, he said to himself that there must be more to life than money.

"But you earn seven figures a year," I had said, still in disbelief that he was walking away from what we had considered the American dream.

"And I don't feel fulfilled," he said. "I feel hollow. I need to feel that I'm making a real difference and not just making rich people richer."

And with that Chris flew off to a small town somewhere in the Midwest and spent the next couple of years studying and preparing for his new mission in life: helping those who were less fortunate.

I didn't know it at the time, but Chris was luckier than the rest of us sitting around the table that afternoon. He had seen the light while the rest of us were trapped in the darkness of this never-ending pursuit of more money, more toys, and more bragging rights. Summer rentals in the outrageously expensive Hamptons, enormous lofts in Tribeca, custom-made suits, cigars smuggled in from Cuba, weekends in Aspen—the more we had, the more we wanted. But we were doing nothing more than amassing things that were only symbols. For many of us, there was no real meaning or substantive purpose to what we were doing. We acquired because we thought it reflected our success, but many of us were secretly unhappy as we sacrificed our true pleasures and time that could've been spent with loved ones. We were living the lives that were expected of us rather than the lives that made us feel whole.

Your Epiphany

Epiphanies tend to occur when you least expect them. An epiphany will startle you, maybe even upend a long-held belief or way of thinking. But don't expect it to happen the way it does in the movies—the Hollywood epiphany where one of the actors is obliviously walking across the street, and a few seconds later two cars collide at the corner where the person had just been standing. Suddenly the character is struck with the deep, insightful understanding that has been eluding him. His life now has meaning and purpose, whether it's to help the starving children in Africa or save the great Amazon jungle from greedy developers.

But epiphanies are rarely brought on by such monumental circumstances. They tend to arrive quietly, and if you're not paying attention, you can easily miss them. Famed psychologist Martin Seligman didn't miss his epiphany, and it forever changed the field of psychology. It was 1998. Seligman had just been elected president of the American Psychological Association, a prestigious post that has been held by some of the country's greatest psychologists. He was in his garden weeding with his five-year-old daughter, Nikki. He readily admits that while he has written books about children, he is not all that good with them one-on-one. He has always been a goal-oriented person and time is urgent when it comes to completing tasks. So when Seligman was weeding that day, he was serious about getting it done efficiently and moving on, just as he was with everything else in his life. Nikki, however, was behaving like any five-year-old: throwing weeds into the air, singing, and dancing around the garden. Seligman yelled at her. She walked away, chastised, and then returned and said that she wanted to talk to him. Her words were prophetic.

Daddy, do you remember my fifth birthday? From the time I was three to the time I was five, I was a whiner. I whined every day. When I turned five, I decided not to whine anymore. That was the hardest thing I've ever done. And if I can stop whining, you can stop being such a grouch.[1]

Seligman goes on to write that that moment was nothing less than an epiphany. Beyond learning something about his daughter and raising kids, he also learned about himself and his profession. He realized that he was a grouch. He wrote:

I had spent 50 years mostly enduring wet weather in my soul, and the past 10 years being a nimbus cloud in a household full of sunshine. Any good fortune I had was probably not due to my grumpiness but in spite of it. In that moment I resolved to change.[2]

And thus was born the modern era of positive psychology, the branch of psychology that studies happiness. For decades psychology had focused on human disease such as depression, bipolar disorder, schizophrenia—what made people sick and how to treat them. But not many researchers were thinking about what it was that made people happy and whether those causes could be applied to others as a road map to happiness.

At first ridiculed as a soft science, positive psychology at-tracted hundreds and then thousands of researchers who pro-duced a growing number of credible studies that confirmed that there was a legitimate reason to study and understand the mechanisms of happiness. Not since the days of Freud had psychology had such buzz, and this buzz wasn't about new medications or cutting-edge methods of analyzing the impaired mind. Rather, it was all about getting behind the smile—work that made even the researchers happy.

1

What Is Happiness?

✧

We tend to forget that happiness doesn't come as a
result of getting something we don't have, but rather of
recognizing and appreciating what we do have.

—FREDERICK KOENIG [1]

What is the definition of happiness? In my search for this slippery answer, I decided to start the old-fashioned way—with the dictionary.

---

n **1**: a state of well-being and contentment; *also*: a
pleasurable satisfaction

MERRIAM-WEBSTER DICTIONARY

Sounds reasonable. But if you line up one hundred psychologists and social scientists and ask them to give their definition, you're likely to get one hundred different answers. And while we tend to like for things to fall into neat little boxes, the definition of happiness certainly doesn't accommodate our desire for neatness. Despite all the research, especially that of the last ten years, and all the advances of those acclaimed positive psychologists who are churning out groundbreaking research, there is no unanimous or *correct* definition of happiness.

What about my own definition of happiness? I know what it feels like, but it takes more effort than I expected to be able to put it into words. I think of different moments of happiness in my life, starting in my early childhood. The first experience that comes to mind is the annual pilgrimage my family made to the Danbury State Fair, an event that always brought great anticipation and joy. Located on more than 130 acres in the southwestern part of Danbury, Connecticut, the fair came to life for seven days every October, and for that one magical week every kid thought our small town was the center of the universe. The fair attracted hundreds of thousands of people from all over Connecticut, New York, and even Massachusetts. Whether it was a chance to ride the giant Ferris wheel, to ogle a 320-pound squash, to watch the sweaty and snorting ox pull, or to fill up on sweet potato pie and cotton candy, the fair was a dream come true for the entire town. In fact, the fair was so important that school was officially closed for one day during that week, and every student was given a free pass to walk through those big gates and explore the rambling grounds. The Danbury State Fair made me not just happy but extremely happy.

Things You'd Assume Would Bring Happiness

Financial security
New car
Big house
Winning the lottery
Nice clothes
Good sex
Success at work
Time away from work
Reading a good book
Acknowledgment from others of your success

As I tried to understand the source of my happiness, I couldn't help but think about the simple and nonmaterialistic events that made my life growing up feel meaningful and engaged. Performing the lead in my Sunday school Christmas and Easter plays, having a perfect attendance record in elementary school, bringing in cans of soup to donate to the holiday food drives, graduating at the top of my class from high school, spending long holidays with my extended family crammed into one house—these were the things that made me happy. Sure, I always wanted to own a fancy house and a luxury car and be able to purchase expensive designer clothes, but as my family's financial position improved through the years and I was able to realize some of these materialistic dreams, one thing became surprisingly clear: The happiness I derived from a coveted sports car and designer clothes was explosive, but the fire burned out relatively quickly. In contrast, nonmaterialistic sources of happiness, such as the plays, family holidays, and soup-can donations, stayed with me for many years. To this day when I think of those times, a warmth overtakes me.

Why did holidays with my family in a cramped house with little in the way of material gifts but lots in the way of love and fun have a more lasting impact on my happiness than the gorgeous and expensive M3 BMW my brother and I were given in our late teens when our family's financial condition improved dramatically? I wanted that car so badly, and when I got to drive it off the lot, I could barely feel my feet on the pedals because I was so full of adrenaline. Not only did

I love the muscular look of the car, but I yearned for the groan of the engine and the stares it brought from drivers and pedestrians alike. But something strange happened about seven months later. It was still a lot of fun to open up the engine on the highway at speeds that were decidedly illegal and unsafe, but I wouldn't say the car was adding to my happiness. Surprisingly, the love affair had cooled.

I wouldn't have been so surprised had I seen the research, which has consistently shown that material-based happiness is transient at best. One famous study looked at lottery jackpot winners and found that their level of happiness five years after receiving their windfall had returned to the same level it had been prior to their winning. If on a scale zero to ten someone's happiness level before the big lottery win was a six, the study showed that for a few years that number jumped, but at the fifth year, regardless of how great the increase, the happiness level returned to a six. An even more revealing study of lottery winners was conducted by Dr. Richard Tunney of the University of Nottingham's School of Psychology in England.[2] Lottery winners were asked how satisfied they were in relation to different parts of their life, how often they treated themselves, and what types of treats they enjoyed. Much to everyone's surprise, it turned out that flashy cars and diamond jewelry weren't responsible for the increased happiness of the jackpot winners, but listening to music, reading a book, or enjoying a good bottle of wine really made a difference. These winners liked rather inexpensive treats: long baths, going swimming, enjoying their hobbies, and having fun playing games.

So what does this say about happiness? The experts suggest that happiness becomes more sustained and impactful because of the characteristics surrounding the experience—meaning, pleasure, and engagement. Martin Seligman, one of the father of positive psychology, defines happiness this way:

> I believe happiness dissolves into three different ideas, each of which is separately buildable and measurable. The first is the (i) pleasant life (having as much positive emotion and as little negative emotion as possible), (ii) the engaged life (being completely absorbed by the challenges you face at work, love, play, etc.), (iii) the meaningful life (knowing what your highest strengths are and using them to belong to and serve something that is bigger than you are).[3]

Seligman's definition—in whole or at least in part—appears to be widely accepted by many leading researchers and thinkers in the field. Former Harvard lecturer, Tal Ben-Shahar, a noted positive psychologist, had this to say on the highly sought-after definition:

> I define happiness as "the overall experience of pleasure and meaning." A happy person enjoys positive emotions

while perceiving her life as purposeful. This definition does not pertain to a single moment, but to a generalized aggregate of one's experiences: a person can endure emotional pain at times and still be happy overall.[4]

Ben-Shahar's definition, taken along with Seligman's, appears to imply a type of philosophical sophistication. Does it mean that if your life isn't Zen-like and purposeful, you can't be happy? Do you have to embark on a mission to do good for mankind or the environment in order to qualify as a happy person? Is there some ranking of what endeavors have the most meaning, thus giving us a guide to the missions that will make us happiest?

Happiness Is a Crowded Dinner Table

Socializing with friends and family is one of the most effective ways to boost happiness. Gathering over a meal is one of the most popular group activities. It makes sense that a good time can be had at a table crowded with loved ones who are sharing stories, laughs, opinions, and even disagreements. In my family it has always been Sunday dinner; regardless of how busy we are, we return home to enjoy not only great food but equally compelling company. Sunday dinners are so important that everyone is careful to schedule activities around them and avoid any conflicts. An empty chair—even in a house full of people—doesn't go unnoticed.

In many ways a crowded dinner table is one big support group with the bonus of good food. In my family there were times when someone was having a tough week. What helped get the person through it was knowing that at the end of the week we'd all be together again, surrounded by love and those who would support us rather than judge us. Equally exciting was sharing good news—a job promotion, academic accomplishment, pregnancy—with those who knew us best and took pride in our successes.

Our Sunday family dinners were so popular that friends would stop by the house unannounced, knowing that there was always an extra seat available at the table and plenty of laughs and warm smiles to make them forget about their troubles or the tough week ahead. Happiness studies have universally shown the power of a strong social network and the positive impact of making our time together meaningful and engaging. Fill up your table and have fun.

In seeking a working definition of happiness, I reexamined the various stages of my life when sadness was rare and happiness and a strong positive attitude really defined who I was. As much as my mother struggled to pay for athletic uniforms,

Things That *Really* Make People Happy

Family, friends, and social companionship

Helping others

Appreciating what you have and not feeling wistful about what you don't have

Making a difference in someone else's life

Pursuing a passion

Taking pride in one's work

Forgiving someone for an offense and moving on

Not trying to keep up with the Joneses

new basketball sneakers, and one book a week from the Weekly Reader, I was every bit as happy as my classmate David Rubin. His father was a doctor, and the Rubin family lived in one of the biggest houses I had ever seen. David had so many toys he could've opened his own store. As I grew older, I met others who had struggled with adversities as children, but these adversities impacted them differently. Some had developed low self-esteem, were constantly depressed, and walked around with a chip on their shoulder. Why did some who were raised in similar circumstances turn out happy while others labored through gloom and pessimism? It wasn't until I started digging into the research on the origins of happiness that I stumbled on part of the answer.

The Happiness Thermostat

Why do some people grow to be only five feet while others grow to be seven feet? Why does one brother have blond hair while the other has red? Why are some children born with type 1 (juvenile) diabetes while others are not? Genes! The DNA in our cells is unique and makes us different from everyone else. What we're going to look like and much of who we have the capacity to become in life has already been scripted in those microscopic genes that we inherit from our parents. And researchers found something similar when they searched for the origins of happiness. A large part of how happy we are or will be is determined by our genetic makeup—something we have no control over.

This is called the "happiness set point." The idea is that we all have a baseline of happiness that represents our resting position when nothing unusually wonderful or unusual is going on in our lives. There are pleasure-inducing situations—buying a new car, celebrating a birthday, receiving a compliment about your appearance—that can make you happier, but this burst in happiness is only temporary. Eventually the "high" you felt will fade away, and you'll return to your normal level of happiness, your happiness set point.

Researchers have tried to figure out how much of the happiness we experience in life is determined before we are born and how much is actually in our control after birth. One of the most famous experts in the study of positive psychology, the late University of Minnesota professor David Lykken, spent years conducting his famous study of fifteen hundred pairs of twins.[5] He concluded that as much as 50 percent of our happiness is determined by our genes (the happiness set point), and the other 50 percent is determined by the circumstances of life. Other prominent researchers such as Sonja Lyubomirsky, Kennon M. Sheldon, and David Schkade built on Lykken's work and found that the 50 percent of happiness attributed to the circumstances of life could be broken down even further.[6]

Intentional activity (under our control) is the biggest chunk and comprises 40 percent. Life's circumstances (not under our control) comprise the final 10 percent.

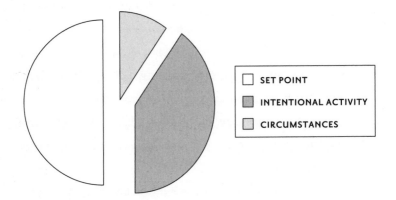

SET POINT

INTENTIONAL ACTIVITY

CIRCUMSTANCES

For those who have believed that they were born unhappy, there is encouraging news: Forty percent of your happiness can be controlled by your actions. Even better, if you get lucky in life, the good things that happen can provide an even greater opportunity for you to achieve some level of lasting happiness. Martin Seligman put it neatly into a formula:

$$H = S + C + V$$

Enduring Happiness (H) = Set point (S) +
Circumstances (C) + Factors Under Voluntary Control (V)

This equation gives us hope that some higher level of happiness is attainable, regardless of where our genes may have predisposed us to be.

Now that we know we have a chance at some higher level of happiness, the $64,000 question then becomes: What do we need to do to make ourselves happier in the long term? We'll discuss some strategies and "happy boosters" in a later chapter, but first it's important to understand what role your genes play in the theater of happiness.

The happiness set point theory is similar to what experts have discovered about weight control. The weight set point theory says that people have a certain weight which is determined by genes, metabolism, and other factors, and it is difficult to change. You might lose weight or gain weight, but the body's natural tendency is to revert to your weight set point. For a long time, I believed that with the proper lifestyle changes people could actually alter their weight set point. Let's say you are a five-foot-five woman, and your weight set point is 150 pounds. It has been argued that with the right exercise and dietary changes sustained over a period of twelve to twenty-four months, you can actually move that set point. It is difficult to predict how far. Can you move it all the way down to 110 pounds? Doubtful. But can you get it down to 135? Absolutely.

Your happiness set point has similar characteristics. Some

people are born with a predisposition to grumpiness or sadness. Something in their genes says that more often than not they will see clouds where others will see blue sky. The good news, however, is that this does not mean they are automatically confined to a sentence of gloom and despair. Just because you have genes that say you have the *potential* to be grumpy and sad doesn't mean that storm clouds are forever in your life's forecast. There still exists the chance that you can learn to see fewer clouds and more blue sky. For some it's a big chance, for others a small chance, but it's a chance nonetheless. While you may not be able to alter your happiness set point as you can your weight set point, you can still have a tremendous impact on your happiness destiny. But there are limits. Someone whose genetics predispose him to being a real grouch is unlikely to be able to alter his happiness set point so far to the positive that he'll be singing and skipping like Mary Poppins. But at least he will be able to feel happier more of the time and not wake up every morning feeling that life is a constant drag.

Lessons from the Happiest People in the World

I was searching for something on the Internet recently when I stumbled across this headline: "And the Happiest Place on Earth Is . . ." I clicked on a video link and watched in sheer amazement when Morley Safer from *60 Minutes* revealed the results of an international study that had been conducted at Leicester University in England.[7] Much to my amazement, the happiest place on Earth was Denmark. *Denmark!* How was that possible? Here was a country of five and a half million people located in northern Europe where the climate isn't the greatest, the people aren't the richest, and the lack of a real military makes it consistently vulnerable to hostile aggression. Then there was an even bigger surprise: The United States was ranked twenty-third, not even in the top ten. Shockingly, it was beaten by such countries as Finland, Costa Rica, and Norway. How could this be?

The report went on to disclose that what put Denmark on top and the United States much lower on the list had to do with expectations. University of Southern Denmark professor Kaare Christensen investigated why his fellow countrymen and -women were so happy. According to Christensen, Danes typically have lower expectations, and this translated into rarely being disappointed.

Americans appear to have a very different attitude about expectations and success. The Danish students who were interviewed in the *60 Minutes* report seemed to have really crystallized this difference. One of them described his measure of success in this way: "I would want to be happy and have a lot of time with my family." A second student said, "It's more about the softer values, such as not being stressed and feeling passionate about what I'm doing. Maybe this job is not going to pay me a lot of money, but I'm going to love getting up and doing it every day."

These are not common American principles. Most of our lives, unless we are fully involved in the care of young children, are centered on the prestige and wages connected to our jobs, and work becomes the dominant force. You can probably find proof of this in your own life. Take a few minutes to sit down and chart your daily schedule by the hour. Most likely the single activity that consumes the largest amount of your time while you're awake is your job. We like to think that the typical work week is forty hours, and for many of us that is true, give or take a couple of hours. But not figured into this math is the amount of time spent traveling to work and coming home from work—essentially adding more time away from your family and doing things you enjoy. According to a 2007 Gallup poll, workers' average round-trip commute is 46 minutes in a typical day. The poll also showed that the longer the commute, the more stressful the commute was to the worker.[8]

In a 2008 Gallup survey, 48 percent of American workers were completely satisfied, while 42 percent were somewhat satisfied, 7 percent somewhat dissatisfied, and 2 percent completely dissatisfied.[9] Some may look at these results and think that they reflect a decent amount of happiness in the workforce, but I read the numbers differently when taken in a broader context. My interpretation is that if a single activity is consuming most of my day, then I want to be completely satisfied with that activity. It's simple: The more time I spend dissatisfied, the less time I can be satisfied, which means decreasing the chances that I will be happy.

What about the money? If you have heard it once, you have heard it a hundred times: "Money can't buy happiness." While the underlying principle of this statement is true, research shows that it is more accurate to say, "Money can buy happiness, but only to a point." It reminds me of one of Mae West's great quips: "I've been rich, and I've been poor. Believe me, rich is better." In most societies those who earn more money tend to be happier than those who don't. There appears to be a minimum amount of money or resources one needs to obtain at least a baseline level of happiness, but what surprises many people is the observation that increasing wealth doesn't always lead to increasing happiness.

A Gallup survey conducted in 2007[10] looked at Americans and their life satisfaction based on several characteristics, including money. Those in the highest income bracket—$75,000 and more—had the highest percentage of happy people at 74 percent. Those in the lowest income bracket—less than $30,000 per year—had the lowest percentage of happy people at 42 percent. You might conclude from this survey that the more money people make, the happier they are, and by increasing your income and net worth, you'll be increasingly happier.

Not so fast. Research shows that money does matter, but only up to a point. Economists and psychologists are quick to point out that while there have been large increases of real income in the developed world over the past fifty years, there hasn't been any real change in reported levels of happiness. Income definitely has a positive relationship to happiness, but it's not the straight line one might expect. When income increases, happiness does not necessarily increase equally.

Inaccurate Relationship Between Money and Happiness

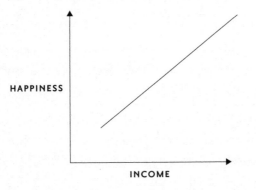

The true relationship is that happiness does increase directly with growing income, but only up to a point. After a certain point (⊕), regardless of how much *more* money you have, your happiness level stays the same.

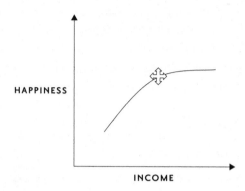

Money can certainly make a difference, especially when you're starting off with a relatively small amount. No one needs millions of dollars to lead a comfortable life, but there is something to be said for attaining some degree of financial independence. Beyond material comforts, this independence can provide many things, including convenience, reducing stress over meeting life's basic needs, and having the ability to donate to worthwhile causes. All these things can increase one's level of happiness. Who doesn't want to earn enough money to eliminate debt, purchase a comfortable home, pay household bills on time, put the children through school without sacrificing lifestyle, and save for retirement? It is important not to overrate the value of money, but it is equally important not to underestimate it, either. Research has shown that much more than a large bank account, being grateful for what you have and showing your

Ways to Say Thank You

Do it the old-fashioned way. Instead of buying a card, create your own thank-you card or write a brief note showing true appreciation.

Surprise someone by remembering and celebrating his or her birthday, wedding anniversary, or other milestone.

Make a donation to a charitable cause in a friend's name.

Give someone a small gift that is relevant to his or her hobby, such as a strip of collectible stamps to a stamp collector.

Take a photo of yourself and the gift you have received, and send it to the giver.

Make it a public thank-you by thanking the recipient in front of a group of his or her peers.

Give someone a year's subscription to a magazine he or she would enjoy. Each time a new issue arrives he or she will think of you.

Give something you have baked. The homemade touch is always valued.

Create a thank-you video. With the low cost and easy access of modern technology, you can videotape your gratitude and send it along.

Rather than giving cut flowers, give someone a small potted plant that will grow over time.

appreciation for the generosity others have bestowed on you can create deeper and longer-lasting happiness.

Own Your Happiness

Achieving ultimate happiness means *owning* it. Too often we allow other people or situations to control our quest for happiness. I have often heard people complain, "My son is making me so unhappy. If only he would do well in school and follow the house rules, I'd be so much happier." Many of my female friends say, "I'd be happy if I could lose weight and find a boyfriend. I'm tired of going home to an empty apartment." A disobedient son, a losing battle against weight gain, and feelings of loneliness understandably make people sad. Disappointments in life are going to happen regardless of how happy you are. But the key is how well you control the impact those disappointments have on your overall happiness.

There are some things in life you can't control. You can be the best parent that ever lived and provide a nurturing and supportive environment for your children, but sometimes a child may strike out on his own and, despite all your teachings, make decisions that lead to trouble and failure. Even with your best and most protective efforts you can't always be there to make decisions for your children. At some point they are going to think and act for themselves. If you tied your entire happiness to the decisions that your child makes, hold on tight because you are in for an emotional roller-coaster ride and long stretches of unhappiness. You have to own your happiness so that the actions or inactions of others don't push you off the road of happiness.

Base your happiness not on an outcome—especially one in which others have some influence—but on your contribution or performance in achieving that outcome. For example, "I'd be happy if my mother would accept me for who I am." If you are the best person you can be and make an honest effort to represent who you really are, then your happiness should be based not on whether someone accepts you but on how honest you are with yourself and others.

Blaming others for your unhappiness is as ineffective as being dependent on others for happiness. Both are surefire recipes for continual disappointment. A critical component of happiness is being realistic. People trying to lose weight face a similar predicament. One of the biggest reasons people feel they fail in a weight-loss journey is unrealistic expectations. They want to lose too much weight too fast, and when they don't reach these overly ambitious goals, they get frustrated and throw the program away. The truth, however, is that the program is likely an effective one, but because the goals are so unrealistic, the dieter unfairly maligns it as a bad plan.

A healthy dose of realism informs us that no one can or should be happy all the time. It is absolutely normal and beneficial to have periods of sadness. Being appropriately sad is part of a healthy emotional existence. Concern should start only when the level or length of sadness is disproportionate to the situation that has caused it or when the intensity of the unhappiness gets in the way of a person's ability to function normally. If you are realistic about what will and should make you happy as well as honest about acknowledging the need to be disappointed and sad in certain situations, then you have a much greater chance of finding stable happiness. Don't feel bad because something happens that upsets you and puts you in a bad mood. The key is how fast you can get through that mood and move into a more positive space.

The Happiness Test

How does one measure happiness? As you might imagine, this isn't an easy task, especially since there is no single definition of happiness. Psychologist Ed Diener and his colleagues at the University of Illinois have created what remains the gold standard when it comes to happiness self-assessment tests. Diener developed the test as a means of measuring "global life satisfaction"—in other words, how happy one is with his or her life. He called the test *Satisfaction with Life Scale*.[11] This simple test typically takes no more than a couple of minutes to complete. It has been used by researchers, clinicians, and coaches throughout the world. How happy are you? Take the test and get an idea.

Below are five statements that you may agree or disagree with. Using the 1–7 scale below, indicate your agreement with each item by placing the appropriate number on the line preceding that item. Please be open and honest in your response.

7—Strongly agree

6—Agree

5—Slightly agree

4—Neither agree nor disagree

3—Slightly disagree

2—Disagree

1—Strongly disagree

_____ In most ways my life is close to my ideal.

_____ The conditions of my life are excellent.

_____ I am satisfied with my life.

_____ So far I have gotten the important things I want in life.

_____ If I could live my life over, I would change almost nothing.

Add up your scores and compare the total to the table below.

- 35–31 Extremely satisfied
- 26–30 Satisfied
- 21–25 Slightly satisfied
- 20 Neutral
- 15–19 Slightly dissatisfied

- 10–14 Dissatisfied
- 5–9 Extremely dissatisfied

YOUR HAPPY PLAN

LIST FIVE THINGS THAT ARE MOST MEANINGFUL IN YOUR LIFE BUT ARE NOT MONEY OR MATERIAL POSSESSIONS.

....

....

....

....

....

TAKE THE FIVE ITEMS YOU LISTED ABOVE AND ESTIMATE THE AMOUNT OF TIME YOU SPEND EACH WEEK DOING THEM, EXPERIENCING THEM, OR THINKING ABOUT THEM.

.... _____ hours per week

.... _____ hours per week

.... _____hours per week

.... _____hours per week

.... _____hours per week

Increase your happiness time! Reorganize your time so there is more allotted for valued activities, people, or places. Go for a goal of at least three to four hours a week for each activity. Sit down with your calendar and chart how you can increase the time you spend on the meaningful activities and decrease the time you spend on the less meaningful activities that are keeping your life unbalanced.

2

Play to Your Strengths

✧

The happiness that is genuinely satisfying is accompanied by the fullest exercise of our faculties and the fullest realization of the world in which we live.

—BERTRAND RUSSELL

Do you know your talents? Do you know your strengths? And do you know the difference between the two? The answers to these three questions can be essential in your quest for happiness. It is all about knowing who you are and finding the best way to apply yourself so that you find success. Playing to your strengths is the best way to handle difficult situations, and by applying your strengths creatively you can increase your happiness and sense of well-being.

Let's start with some basic definitions. According to leading positive psychologists, moral traits such as integrity, fairness, and loyalty are strengths. Talents such as artistic ability, athletic ability, and music ability don't have anything to do with moral traits. Both talents and traits are qualities that can be enhanced and built on in a significant way. However, you can do more with moral traits than with talents: You can become dramatically braver and more creative in your approach to life. When it comes to talent, you can improve on your ability to make baskets or kick goals on a soccer field, but the level of improvement may not be significant when compared to your baseline abilities. Talents are largely innate; they are abilities brought to the surface as we begin to use them when pursuing various activities. For example, some children even as young as two have naturally good eye-hand coordination, which makes them very good at being able do such things as hit a baseball that has been thrown to them. While in rough form, this talent through practice can be polished to the point of exceptional ability. Strengths, on the other hand, are personality traits that can be *acquired* through active intentions such as practicing, reading, or learning from teachers. Just because we were not born with certain personality traits doesn't mean we can't develop them. For example, you can train yourself to be diligent, to learn how to finish something you start rather than drift off to other interests before the task at hand is complete.

Lastly, there is a big difference between talent and strengths when it comes to choice. There are many more choices when it comes to strengths. You can *decide* whether you want to have a particular strength, whether you want to develop the strength even further, and whether you want to use that strength. If you believe that talent is largely innate, then essentially it is something that you don't have a lot of control over.

Understanding your strengths is important because research has shown that one way to increase your happiness and life success is to spend more time using those strengths. The leading psychological researcher Richard Sternberg from Tufts University developed a revolutionary concept called "successful intelligence." His premise is quite simple. We should spend as little time as possible on our weaknesses and most of our time on our strengths. He found that people who are most successful aren't necessarily those who have the highest IQs or GPAs. Instead they are people who know who they are, who know what they're good at, and who work on developing and employing those strengths.

Researchers were careful to look into this question of what happens when people not only identify their signature character strengths but also use them in a new way.[1] For example, if forgiveness is one of your signature strengths, you probably show or express it by telling yourself and the other person that you forgive them. One way to be creative is to not just tell them that you forgive them, but actually go further and do something nice for them or give them a small gift. Researchers found that not only did happiness increase and depressive symptoms decrease, but this positive effect lasted up to six months. The key is to identify your five greatest strengths and develop them.

A prestigious group of social scientists and psychologists, including Martin Seligman and Christopher Peterson, wanted to standardize the concepts of virtue and strengths. They looked across three thousand years of cultures and religions and tried to identify the core virtues that can be found in almost all of them. These six universal virtues were wisdom, courage, humanity, justice, temperance, and transcendence. Taken together, these virtues comprise the concept of good character. But how do we as individuals achieve these virtues in our life? This is where our strengths enter in and play a leading role. We achieve these virtues through our strengths of character. Twenty-four signature strengths have been defined and accepted. You might find that ten or fourteen or seventeen in some way apply to you, but the key is to figure out which ones apply to you more than the others do. Read below for how the six virtues are defined and to see which of the entries sound *most* like you, and you'll find your five signature strengths.

THE VIRTUE OF WISDOM

STRENGTHS

1. Curiosity/Interest in the World

You are not hung up with preconceptions. You are open to new experiences, and you take a flexible approach to things. You just don't tolerate ambiguity but even are intrigued by it and like it. You like to explore and discover.

2. Love of Learning

You have a love for learning new things, whether it is in a formal setting, such as a class or seminar, or informally on your own. Possessing knowledge and mastery of a topic excite you. You enjoy being an expert in a particular field and/or being in a position where your knowledge is valued by others. Your learning is not incentivized by any external reward it will bring; rather, you enjoy learning for the sake of learning.

3. Judgment/Critical Thinking/Open-mindedness

You are a deliberate thinker, someone who doesn't rush to judgment. You take your time to think things through carefully. You examine issues from all sides and make decisions based on reliable evidence that you weigh fairly. You are not someone who locks into an unchangeable position. If the evidence contradicts a previous position you've taken or are currently taking, you are willing to change your mind.

4. Ingenuity/Originality/Practical Intelligence/Street Smarts

You rarely settle for doing things the conventional way. You excel in finding new and different ways to approach problems and/or to achieve goals.

5. Perspective

This is the strength closest to wisdom. You are sought after by others who want to use your experience to help them solve problems and gain perspective. Your way of looking at the world makes sense not only to yourself but to others as well.

6. Social Intelligence/Personal Intelligence/Emotional Intelligence

You possess a good understanding of yourself and others. Not only do you have an awareness of the motives and feelings of others, but you can respond well to them. You are very good at judging moods, temperament, motivations, and intentions and responding appropriately. You are in touch with your own feelings, and because of this you can understand and guide your own behavior. You also have the keen ability to put yourself in settings that maximize your skills and interests. You choose your work, your intimate relations, and your leisure to put your best abilities into play every day.

THE VIRTUE OF COURAGE

STRENGTHS

1. Bravery and Valor

You don't back down or succumb to threats, difficulty, challenge, or pain. Even when certain situations are unpopular or dangerous, you are prepared to take them on. Your bravery is also evident in your ability to overcome fear. When faced with danger or a perceived threat, the normal reaction is "fight or flight." You are someone who resists the urge to flee; instead, you stay and deal with the fearful situation. Valor, among other things, refers to moral and psychological courage. Moral courage means a willingness to take stances that are unpopular and likely to come at a cost. Psychological courage includes the stoic and even cheerful stance needed to face trying situations.

2. Perseverance/Industry/Diligence

You are someone who finishes what you start. You take on difficult projects, not only finishing them but doing so with a positive attitude and few complaints. You do what you say you're going to do, and sometimes you do more. You are determined to reach your goals, but you're reasonable and don't let your goals turn into blinding obsessions. You are flexible, realistic, and ambitious.

3. Integrity/Genuineness/Honesty

You are an honest person, not only in telling the truth but in how you live your life. You make your intentions known, and you honor your commitments. You are someone who is down to earth and relatable as well as genuine and authentic. You live without pretense.

THE VIRTUE OF
HUMANITY AND LOVE

STRENGTHS

I. Kindness and Generosity

You are kind and generous to others and try your hardest to do favors for those who request them. Doing good deeds for others gives you pleasure and joy. You realize that others should be respected, and you believe others also have worth. This leads you to consider their best interests in your decision-making even when your personal desires might be in conflict.

2. Loving and Allowing Oneself to Be Loved

You place a high value on close relationships with others. Those whom you have deep feelings about feel the same way toward you. What is also important is that you allow yourself to be loved.

THE VIRTUE OF JUSTICE

STRENGTHS

1. Citizenship/Duty/Teamwork/Loyalty

You are a reliable teammate who functions very well in a group. Loyalty and dedication are attributes that make you an excellent team member. You don't depend on others to do your portion; you carry your own load. You work hard, even going the extra distance sometimes to bring success to the group. There is a saying, "There's no *I* in team." You embrace this philosophy and thrive in collaborative relationships.

2. Leadership

You're a good organizer, and you make sure that plans are carried out. You're able to promote and keep good relations between group members while being an effective leader. You are also skilled at handling relations between your group and others.

3. Fairness and Equity

You are able to keep your personal feelings and possible prejudices in check and not allow them to bias your decisions about other people. You give everyone a fair chance and allow your larger principles of morality to guide you. The welfare of others, even if they're strangers, is as important to you as your own well-being.

THE VIRTUE OF TEMPERANCE

STRENGTHS

1. Prudence/Discretion/Caution

You are a careful person and look before you leap. You avoid saying or doing things that you might later regret. You typically wait until all options have been fully considered before taking any course of action. You are able to look ahead by resisting impulses for the sake of longer-term success.

2. Humility and Modesty

You neither seek nor want the spotlight but instead prefer to let your accomplishments speak for themselves. You don't see yourself as special, and others comment on and respect your modesty. Your humility allows you to see your personal aspirations, successes, and failures as relatively unimportant.

3. Self-control

You are well disciplined and can easily hold your desires, needs, and impulses in check when necessary or appropriate. When something bad happens, you are able to control your emotions and even cheer yourself up when facing a difficult situation. You are able to turn around and neutralize your negative feelings.

THE VIRTUE OF TRANSCENDENCE

STRENGTHS

I. Gratitude

You are aware of good things that happen to you, both small and large, and you don't take them for granted. You take the time to express your thanks, and you appreciate the goodness you find in others.

2. Hope/Optimism/Future-mindedness

You have a positive outlook for the future and expect good things to happen. Not only do you think the best is yet to come, but you plan and work in order to make it happen. You lead a goal-directed life with a focus on the future.

3. Appreciation of Beauty and Excellence

You take your time to appreciate and enjoy the good things in life. You are the type of person who appreciates beauty, excellence, and skill across various spheres in life, whether it be sports, singing, art, or intellectual pursuits.

4. Forgiveness and Mercy

If you are wronged, you are able to forgive. You give people a second chance. Your actions tend to be guided more by mercy than revenge. You not only forgive those who have offended you but are able to show them empathy and compassion.

5. Playfulness and Humor

You enjoy a good laugh, and it pleases you to make others smile. You don't take yourself or life too seriously. You enjoy taking a break from work to play.

6. Zest/Passion/Enthusiasm

You are someone who is energetic, spirited, and passionate. When you do something, you go full steam ahead. You wake up in the morning excited about the new day and look forward to what's coming. Others can feel your passion.

7. Spirituality/Sense of Purpose/Faith/Religiousness

You strongly believe there is a higher purpose and meaning in the universe. You recognize and accept that while your life is important, there is a bigger force than you. You are aware of your position in the world and in the larger scheme of things. Your beliefs guide your actions and provide comfort.

Sometimes we have to find a way to use our strengths creatively. For example, those who are strong in leadership and fairness could find themselves in a nonfulfilling job that doesn't tap into those strengths. They might take the initiative to form a committee that looks at employee complaints (leadership) and discuss them constructively with management (fairness). Those with the traits of persistence and kindness might decide to help a nonprofit raise money for the various programs it supports. Finding a way to make use of your strengths will not only add more meaning to your life but boost your level of happiness.

A. IDENTIFY AND LIST YOUR FIVE GREATEST STRENGTHS.

....

....

....

....

....

B. TAKE EACH OF THE STRENGTHS LISTED ABOVE AND LIST ONE WAY YOU CAN TRY TO USE IT IN YOUR EVERYDAY AND/OR WORK LIFE.

....

....

....

....

....

C. LIST AT LEAST ONE GOAL YOU HOPE TO ACHIEVE FOR EACH OF THE FIVE STRENGTHS LISTED ABOVE.

....

....

....

....

....

3

The Silver Lining

✦

*A pessimist sees the difficulty in every opportunity; an optimist
sees the opportunity in every difficulty.*

—WINSTON CHURCHILL

The Glass Is Half Full

For as long as I can remember I have been an optimist. I was
optimistic before I even knew what the word meant. When
others focused on the clouds, I paid attention to whether there

was any blue between the gaps. It was my signal that the rain—if it did come—would not last forever. I wish I could boast that this early positive thinking was something that came naturally to me, as if I could perceive things well beyond my years. The truth, however, is that life's realities taught me the importance of positive thinking.

One of the most devastating realizations for any boy is the awareness that he is fatherless. Even now I can vividly remember those occasions that intruded on my otherwise pleasant childhood—occasions when I stumbled upon this explosive reality. Each time was like finding a land mine buried in a field of bright dandelions. One of my earliest memories of it was in elementary school. It was that time of year when report cards were being sent home—a major event in my small town where education was a top priority. Academic achievement was extremely important to my hardworking family. It was instilled in me at a young age that learning vast amounts of information and performing well in the classroom would be my best chance at attaining success in life. Believing in the family mantra, I worked hard to learn everything I could and to master those skills that were necessary for peak academic performance. When report cards were distributed, it was like taking home a trophy after a hard-fought championship series. My grades were impeccable and consistently placed me at the top of the class. I was proud because my mother, grandparents, aunts, and uncles were proud. I was too young to really grasp what academic prowess could mean for my life, but I still plowed ahead toward excellence with the assurance from my family that this was the right and only thing to do.

At the end of one marking period in first grade, it was time for my report card to come home to my family. There was a place on the back of the report card envelope for parents to sign—verification that we had actually brought the card home and that it had been reviewed. Once the envelope was signed, we would take it back to school and hand it to our teacher. I had gotten a great report card—all E's (Excellent) and one VG (Very good)—and I was thrilled that I would be handing it to my mother, who I knew would swallow me with one of her enormous hugs. Then she would hand the report card to my grandparents, and the rotation would begin in earnest. We passed report cards around in my family the way other people do newborns. Everyone got their time to touch and feel and enjoy. But as I examined the envelope that afternoon, I realized there was a place for both a mother's signature and a father's signature. That was a big problem, at least in the mind of a six-year-old. I didn't have a father. He had walked out on us unceremoniously when I was just shy of my second birthday. My agonizing dilemma: Who was going to sign on the back of the report card envelope where my father was supposed to sign? If there was no signature in that slot, did that mean the report card and my hard-earned grades wouldn't count? I didn't exactly cry that afternoon, but I was scared and angry and embarrassed. Why was I in this situation? Why couldn't I have a mother and father at home like Susan De-Franco? Both of her parents were there not only to sign her report card but also to attend school functions such as plays and the parent-teacher conferences? What was I going to do?

My mother eventually discovered my distress, which I had unsuccessfully tried to hide. She calmly explained to me that her signature was enough, and not having a father's signature wouldn't make the report card worth less. Plenty of other little boys and girls would also have only one signature. As always, my mother made everything perfectly right. With my confidence restored, I proudly returned that envelope with just her signature, knowing I had accomplished something that had made my entire family feel special. I was immensely happy and chalked up the part about not having a father as the way things were that I could do nothing about. I was determined to succeed despite his absence. My grandmother put it best: "It is what it is. Now we move on."

Optimism was my way of dealing with some of life's early hard knocks. I convinced myself that regardless of how much the odds were stacked against me, things would get better if I continued to do well in school, obey my mother, go to church, and never place myself on the wrong side of the law. I didn't understand pessimism because there simply was no room for it in my quest for personal improvement and success. I believed that if I worked hard enough and concentrated, I could win at anything, whether it was a schoolyard game of hopscotch or a statewide chess tournament.

Unfortunately, many people misunderstand optimism. They think that someone who is optimistic is always happy and never gets discouraged. That is simply not the case. An optimist is someone who can look at a situation, assess it for what it really is, and if it's negative, find a way to see at least parts of it in a positive light. Optimists tend to explain positive events as having happened because of them, not because of some random outside force. For example, if you met and networked with an important business contact at a party, the optimistic view is that you were smart to go to that party. The pessimistic view would be that you were just in the right place at the right time, and thanks to luck you were able to make the contact.

Conversely, optimists don't see negative events as being due to their own behavior or decision making. In fact, they see negative events as *not* being their fault and as isolated occurrences. For example, let's say you own a small business, and at the end of the month your sales weren't high enough for you to cover your monthly expenses. The optimistic view is that despite all your hard work and planning, it was a slow month for business, but things will get better in the future as the economy rebounds. The pessimistic view would be to think: "I'm an awful salesperson and poor business manager. The business won't get better because I'm not smart enough to turn things around. Soon I'll have to close my doors."

An optimist—as I learned from my own early experiences—is positioned well to meet success. Negative situations and results are more likely to roll off your back, and rather than drag you down psychologically, you shake off the bad experience and prepare for something more positive. Optimists are better positioned to grab productive opportunities. Optimists believe in their ability to make good things happen, and their central credo is that there is more good than bad in life.

It Pays to Be Optimistic

Optimists are happier people in all realms of life. Years of empirical research had shown this to be true. Unfortunately, many people dismiss optimism as some soft, fuzzy, deluded perspective that is out of touch with reality and delivers little in the way of tangible benefits. Some have even gone so far as to argue that optimism is nothing more than a sham to make people feel better about their undesirable circumstances. But despite these efforts to deny the powers of optimism, one needs to look no further than the mound of scientific research that clearly illustrates the wide breadth of its benefits. Optimists are happier simply because life doesn't knock them around and bruise them the way it does pessimists. Going one step further, the positive disposition of the typical optimist also means that the impact of life's difficult situations hits less and doesn't last as long as it does for those saddled with a gloomy outlook. Here is what the research on optimism has shown:

The Benefits of Optimism

Optimists are persistent and believe that adversities can be overcome.
Optimists are healthier.
Optimists bounce back more quickly from rejection and setbacks.
Optimists tend to be more productive on the job.
Optimists try harder because they believe they have real control over the outcome of events.
Optimists believe they will frequently achieve success.
Optimists are less likely to quit their jobs.
Optimists handle change better, which allows them to adjust to a changing environment.

Optimists live longer. Many studies have examined this issue: one of the most convincing was conducted at the preeminent Mayo Clinic.[1] Between the years 1962 and 1965 researchers asked more than eleven hundred patients to complete a personality survey that gave them an optimism ranking based on their view of the causes of events in their lives. The researchers then went back to those same patients thirty years later. Those who had been classified as optimists had a 19 percent higher chance of still being alive than the pessimists. The study also showed that optimists were less likely to suffer depression and helplessness and were more positive about their health choices.

More recently a nine-year study in the Netherlands divided nine hundred people into two groups—optimists and pessimists—so that researchers could follow their health outcomes.[2] The data showed convincingly that for all causes of death, optimists fared better than pessimists, with an astounding 55 percent lower risk of death. These results added to the growing evidence that there is something real about the links between our mind, body, and attitude and life's quality and duration.

Optimists perform better. No one in the world expected the New York Giants football team to have a chance against the New England Patriots in 2008's Super Bowl XLII. No one, that is, except the Giants, their families and friends, and their diehard fans. The New England Patriots, led by the seemingly invincible quarterback Tom Brady, had just finished a historic undefeated regular season and had proven that they would go down as one of the greatest teams ever—especially if they could also win the Super Bowl in the same year. Only one other team in the history of the sport had ever gone undefeated through the regular season and playoffs and then went on to win the Super Bowl. Every sports pundit on television and every bookie in Vegas had had fiercely predicted the Patriots as the second team to accomplish such a heroic feat—and with good reason. Man for man the Patriots were a better team than the Giants, and throughout the regular season they had demolished their opponents even when they weren't playing their best. There was every reason to believe that the Patriots would defeat the Giants and claim their place in history—every reason *except* for the Giants' power of optimism.

One of my best friends, Michael Strahan, played defensive end for the Giants. We often spoke right before his games, and I would share with him a motivational quote or thought to get him pumped up before he took the field. The day of the Super Bowl, the biggest game of his long career, was no different. My message to him, which he was to deliver to the team in their pregame hype session, was to *believe*. They could win this game if they believed in themselves and their abilities. Forget what everyone else in the country was saying on television and sports radio and in newspaper columns. If the Giants *believed* they could win, then they had a really good chance of bringing the Lombardi trophy home to New York City.

I could hear in his voice that morning that he believed it could happen. It wasn't simply one of those "be positive against the odds" tones. He *really* believed they could beat the Patriots, and his level of optimism was palpable as he explained to me why.

My brother and I were lucky enough to have tickets for the game. We got to the stadium early enough to see the teams' pregame warmups. The second the Giants ran onto the field, I could tell they really believed they could win. You can often see defeat in the way a player walks, drops his shoulders, or responds to the fans. The Giants came on the field that afternoon with a swagger that said, *"Doubters be damned. We are going to win this game."*

After sixty hard-fought minutes that had the entire arena on its feet almost the entire time, the New York Giants did the "impossible" and beat the New England Patriots by a score of 17–14 on a magical play during the last minute of the game. With a super dose of optimism driving them, many of the New York players turned in extraordinary performances, and one of the greatest Super Bowl upsets entered the record books.

To many psychologists and researchers who study the power of optimism, this result was not as surprising as it might seem. In fact, studies have looked at optimistic athletes and the impact that their positive outlook had on their performance. One such study involved swimmers.[3] Researchers enlisted thirty-three male and female members of the swim teams at the University of California at Berkeley. All the swimmers answered a questionnaire that allowed the researchers to determine if they were optimistic or pessimistic. At a team practice they were asked to swim their best event as fast as possible, but instead of giving them their real times when they finished, the researchers gave them false times. The swimmers would therefore be disappointed and think they swam slower than they actually had. According to optimism theory, those who were optimistic would have a positive outlook for the future when presented with a disappointing result. Optimists would try harder the next time and likely do better on the second swim trial. If not, at least they wouldn't do any worse. The researchers predicted a different outcome for the pessimistic swimmers, however. The pessimists would feel that there was little they could do to improve their time and thus wouldn't try harder on the second trial. Their second set of times would not be better.

The results showed that the optimists did about as well on the second trial as they had done on the first, but the pessimists performed even worse. The researchers believed this affirmed pessimism theory—those who expect a negative event don't try to avoid it, and thus the negative event occurs. Optimists always believe there is a chance they can win or do better, and thus they are persistent in trying to bring about that positive outcome. The New York Giants were optimistic about winning Super Bowl XLII, and despite the odds stacked against them, they won the championship and brought the Lombardi trophy home to New York.

Optimists feel less stress. At the core of an optimist's existence is his belief in himself and his abilities. This belief leads an optimist to expect that good things will happen in the future. Life isn't always a "bed of roses," and negative things do happen to optimists. But because the optimist views these negative events as minor setbacks that can be overcome, he

Ways to Turn a Bad Day into a Good One

Write a letter to someone who has affected your life and thank the person for all he or she has done.

Pray and/or meditate and remind yourself of all the opportunities that life offers. Mentally, make difficult situations temporary and acknowledge that they will eventually go away. Instead, focus on the more positive things that you have to look forward to.

Pick a favorite song to play and sing along with it. It is not easy to be sad when you're singing to music that makes you happy.

Commit an act of kindness and do something for someone you love. Bask in the smile on that person's face and his cheer-fulness.

Play with children. The natural happiness and silliness of children can be contagious. They'll make you see the world in a new way.

Count your blessings. Life isn't always perfect, and there are moments of sadness and difficulty, but think about all the things that have gone right in your life. Try to list five of them.

Call the most uplifting and positive person you know. Conversing with someone who has a positive outlook can put those bad moments or situations in perspective.

Do some type of physical activity. Release those endorphins—happy chemicals—into your bloodstream.

Play with your pet if you have one. Pets, especially dogs, offer unconditional love.

Look at the bigger picture. Think about this being only one day of your life and all the other days you have ahead of you that will be meaningful and happy. Don't allow yourself to be stalled by a day that, however challenging, will be over with the next sunrise.

rarely feels the full brunt of stress and anxiety. He can look forward to the positive future to diminish the present impact of the negative event. Someone who constantly sees and focuses on the bad events and believes his future will be full of unfortunate circumstances feels the full weight of the stress that this gloomy outlook will bring.

Optimists as Realists

My college, like most colleges, was a fertile ground for debate. In fact, a good chunk of our learning didn't happen in those storied lecture theaters and steaming laboratories but, rather, in the Freshman Union crowded around the dining hall tables with other students. It was in those relaxed environments that you could find someone who spent the summer in Malawi helping to build schools, sandwiched between someone whose father hauled garbage and another classmate who went home for holidays and regularly dined with U.S. senators and Supreme Court justices. Different backgrounds and experiences inevitably led to different perspectives and opinions, and these differences were the true educational fiber that held us together.

One night we were sitting in the dining hall, and after eating the bulk of our meal, we did what we typically did: pushed our trays aside and sat back to digest whatever thoughts came to mind. Sometimes we debated sports or who was the sexiest movie star, but this night the topic was something much weightier and divisive: politics. Andrew Thorpe, son of a staunchly conservative wealthy family that had been Washington, D.C., insiders for years, squared off against Jeremiah Steinholtz, a New York City upper West Sider who could always find a thread of good even in the most dire of circumstances. Thorpe and Steinholtz volleyed fiercely as they debated everything from social welfare programs to the impact of privatization of governmental services (such as the post office). I don't remember a lot of what they had said that night, but I do remember a point in the debate when it turned personal. Thorpe accused Steinholtz of being a "bleeding liberal" and, even worse, an "eternal optimist." Thorpe insisted that his own ideas were rooted in not only intellectual honesty but realism. "You're a foolish optimist," he seethed. "And I'm a realist."

When I studied optimism theory years later, I realized how flawed Thorpe's concluding statement had been. Thorpe set up realism and optimism as two opposites, as diametrically opposed as hot and cold or black and white. But that is not so. The proper polar opposites are optimists and pessimists, not optimists and realists. In fact, I believe that both optimists and pessimists can be realists to a degree. The difference, however, is how they see that famous glass—either half full or half empty. Not all optimists are realistic, and not all pessimists are realistic. Instead there exists a subset of both that are realistic and yet still differ in how they see the "realities" of the world.

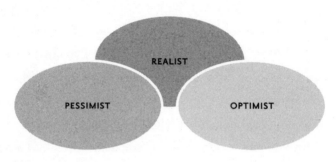

While optimists tend to be hopeful of positive outcomes, sometimes they can be unrealistic. Take the world of professional sprinting, for example, where major progress is recorded by tenths of a second. Although it doesn't appear to be much of a difference, going from a time of 9.9 to 9.8 in the 100-meter sprint is not only difficult but considered quite an accomplishment. Now take a sprinter, Chad Fox, who has never run the 100-meter in better than 11 seconds. He is competing in a race with runners far more talented who consistently run the race in under 10 seconds. Fox can be optimistic that he will break the 11-second barrier, though he has never done it before, but it would be completely unrealistic to think that he could suddenly run fast enough to break the world record of 9.58. Not all optimists are realistic, and there are those who have much higher expectations than are reasonable.

Look at the pessimists. Let's say the country is facing tough economic times and all the indicators point to a period of difficulty. The unemployment rate is up, the Gross Domestic Product (GDP) is down, the inflation rate is up, new homes sales are down, and merchants' retail numbers have declined for two consecutive quarters. The realistic pessimist would say that the economy is in tough times, that individuals are going to feel the squeeze, and that it will take some time and hard work to change things around. The unrealistic pessimist would say that the economy will never get better and that the entire system of capitalism needs to be overhauled to change things around before it completely collapses. Pessimists—like optimists—can be either realistic or unrealistic.

Optimism Is Built into Our Brains

We are born optimistic creatures. In science speak, we're "hard-wired" to be optimists. Researchers believe that our brains have been constructed in a way that leads us to believe the future is going to be better than the past even when there is no evidence to support such expectations. In general we tend to expect to live longer than the average life expectancy, we underestimate the likelihood of getting a divorce, and we underestimate costs and overestimate benefits when planning a project. This is what is called optimism bias—the demonstrated systemic tendency for people to be overly optimistic about the outcome of planned actions. It is in our nature to overestimate the likelihood of positive events and underestimate the likelihood of negative events. Why do we do this?

A small study done at New York University tried to answer that question.[4] Fifteen optimistic volunteers were placed in a brain scanner. Once inside the scanner, the volunteers had to perform several mental functions. They were asked to recall a negative event in the past, imagine what it would be like to be involved in a car crash in the near future, and reflect on positive events such as winning an award in the past or receiving a large amount of cash in the future. As the participants performed each of these individual thoughts, their brains were scanned using a special MRI called a functional MRI.

The study showed that when the volunteers reflected on past and future events, two areas deep in the midbrain lit up on the screen, evidence that there was increased activity in those regions—the amygdala and the rostral anterior cingulated cortex (rACC). What was more telling was that when the volunteers imagined positive events in the future, there was a significantly bigger brain response than when they thought about negative events. The researchers also found that when compared to the optimists, the pessimists in the group had less activity in these regions when they imagined happy events.

We all have these areas in our brain—nature's way of saying that we are built to see the glass half full. But what is not well understood is why some of us still lean toward the pessimistic view of seeing the glass half empty.

Learning Optimism

The good news is that years of research have demonstrated that if you're not an optimist, you can learn how to become one. Following are some basic concepts and principles. When you begin to practice them, they will have an immediate effect on how you see the world, and you will derive benefits from this new outlook on life.

Let us first take a look at how an optimist sees the world versus how a pessimist might. Remember, how we see events influences how we interpret them, and this impacts how we respond to the event. Many noted psychologists talk about the importance of how people explain the good and bad events in their lives. They call this "explanatory style," and it is the basis of how you can begin to change your way of thinking and move toward optimism. This chart will help you grasp the basic concept.

	HOW GOOD EVENTS ARE DESCRIBED	HOW BAD EVENTS ARE DESCRIBED
Optimist	Permanent: They are responsible and predictors of more good events	Temporary: outside of their control and unlikely to happen again
Pessimist	Temporary: outside of their control and unlikely to happen again	Permanent: They are responsible and predictors of more bad events

So how does someone who tends toward pessimism move in the direction of optimism? According to the most widely accepted research, it is all about being able to change the way you make sense of the events that happen in your life. Psychologists like to call this the "appraisal process." According to the cognitive behavioral theory, how you think about what is happening to you actually influences how you feel and respond. A technique called "cognitive restructuring" or "cognitive reframing" trains you to learn how to recognize and fix the errors in your thinking. For example, let's say you're sitting on a city bus going home from work; you're tired and looking forward to a relaxing and pleasant night. Your attention is occasionally drawn to what is happening inside the bus such as an elderly woman walking with a cane and needing help to get to her seat or a group of teenagers listening to music on their iPods and laughing at something only they can hear and understand. The bus eventually fills up, and the only seat open is the one next to you. At the next stop several new passengers board, but instead of sitting next to you, they walk by and decide to stand.

The pessimist might say, "These people don't want to take this seat next to me because there's something wrong with the way I look." The optimist might say, "They didn't take the empty seat because they simply didn't see it, or they're getting off soon and don't want to sit down for such a short ride."

Cognitive restructuring teaches you how to take control of your thought process and fix the mental errors that lead you to a distorted interpretation of the events or circumstances you experience. For the example above we would create a "thought record" that might go something like this:

Identify the Event	Isolated on a Crowded City Bus
Thoughts going through your mind associated with the event	I'm unattractive. My clothes make me look weird. I smell funny.
How do these thoughts make you feel?	Sad Rejected Lonely Foolish
Objective evidence that supports your thoughts	None

(Continued)

Identify the Event	Isolated on a Crowded City Bus
Alternative ways of thinking about the event (a revision of the thoughts above)	They didn't see the open seat. They had been sitting most of the day and wanted to stand. They would rather leave it available for someone who was elderly or physically challenged.
How do you feel after "fixing" your original thoughts?	Foolish for automatically assuming bad things about myself. I'm too hard on myself. I jump to negative conclusions too fast.

This is an exercise that you can do on your own, but remember that repetition and honesty are critical for it to make a difference. The goal is to identify the errors in thought that you make initially to fix the errors and to understand the feelings that are attached to both the original thoughts and the fixes. The more you repeat this exercise, the less often you'll make the initial errors in thought. Instead of seeing life through the lens of negativity, you will now be peering through the rose-colored lens of optimism. Just because you're an optimist doesn't mean that life won't contain some stormy clouds. But at least with optimism on your side you'll be able to find that silver lining and know that blue skies are in the coming forecast.

YOUR
HAPPY
PLAN

A. List seven events or situations that have disappointed you recently.

....

....

....

....

....

....

....

B. Take the seven items listed above and find something positive in each of them.

....

....

....

....

....

....

....

Find the positive.

Every day take a situation that has disappointed you and look for one positive thing in it. The more you practice, the more likely a positive perspective will naturally become part of your life.

4

Simplicity Is Bliss

✧

Simplicity is the ultimate sophistication.
—LEONARDO DA VINCI

*Reduce the complexity of life by eliminating the needless wants
of life, and the labors of life reduce themselves.*
—EDWIN WAY TEALE

As a young medical resident in my fourth year of training, I
was working in a nursing home on Staten Island, one of the
five boroughs of New York City. All my patients during this
two-month rotation were elderly, and many of them had been
dumped into this facility and forgotten. Abandonment has

long been one of the greatest fears of the aging. I always saved my favorite patient for last so that I could spend a few extra minutes visiting with him.

"How are you feeling today, Mr. Holmes?" I asked. Emmerson Holmes was an emaciated ninety-nine-year-old man who had lived on his own up until he developed shingles—the adult variant of chicken pox that is extremely painful and sometimes difficult to effectively treat.

"I've felt better, and I've felt worse," he said. "But why complain when there are thousands of people who are gonna meet their Maker today? I hope I won't be one of them."

I immediately noticed that he wasn't his typically cheerful self. I could hear it in his voice and see it in his body language.

"If I could get you anything in the world you wanted to make you happy, what would it be?" I asked.

Mr. Holmes turned back from the window and looked up at me as I stood over his bed. The sunlight spontaneously danced off his glasses and made his gray eyes look like crushed glass. He released one of his slow smiles that started with just a quiver from the dimple in his chin and spread almost to his ears.

"Anything in the world," he repeated quietly to himself. "That's quite a tall order."

"Try me," I said. I was certain he would say something like money or to be thirty-five again or maybe even a special type of food that he missed after being in the nursing home for so long. The food the patients were served was definitely not the highlight of their stay.

"Nothing extravagant," he said, turning back toward the window, his face totally washed out by the sun. "Something simple. I'd like to see my children and grandchildren. I'd like them to visit me so that I can tell them how much I miss and love them—especially the little ones. I don't want them to forget me."

"Why don't they come to see you?" I asked.

"Because everyone is so busy," he said, his voice starting to quiver. "They have a lot more important things to do in life than see an old man sitting in a nursing home waiting to die."

The anguished look on Mr. Holmes's face that afternoon and the longing in his words have stayed with me all these years. Here was a man nearing the end of a full life, isolated and wasting away in a crowded home, and all he wanted was to spend some time with those he loved most. Sometimes the simple things truly are what matter most.

So much of our life is unnecessarily cluttered with extraneous and meaningless noise that drowns out the more melodious harmonies that resonate so much more deeply. Take a few minutes and think about your own life and how crammed it is with stuff. E-mails, BlackBerries, Twitter tweets, meetings, shopping—our days are consumed by a continuous stream of activity, most of it mundane and uninspiring. Then when we've become exhausted, we collapse in our beds or on the sofa with the television staring back at us, only to wake up the next morning to spin the wheel all over again. The lesson to be learned is simple. Too many dark clouds can block the most beautiful sunset. Less is often more, and simplifying your life isn't as difficult or as painful as you might think.

Anonymous Acts of Kindness

Donate a coat to a winter coat drive.

Help prepare meals for a program such as Meals on Wheels.

Plant flowers in a neighborhood that needs some rejuvenation.

Leave a toy in front of the door of a family that has children.

Send a small box of school or art supplies to a school in your neighborhood.

Collect some of your books that are in good condition and drop them off at your local library.

Send a care package to someone overseas in the armed forces.

Purchase several pieces of infant clothing and donate them to a shelter.

Drop off a computer you no longer use at a community center.

Feed someone else's parking meter that has expired or is almost out of time.

Tape some money to a vending machine with a note that it's for anyone who is short on change.

Pay the bill for an individual or family dining in the same restaurant.

Five Things to Simplify Your Life

1. Digital Declutter

With the advances of technology, e-mail, and various other communication devices, our lives have become one big connection with the switch always turned to the "on" position. Many of us are drowning in digital clutter and don't even know it. I had my first realization of how bad it had gotten one unfortunate afternoon in the middle of rainy New York City. I had just finished having lunch with an editor friend of mine and was heading back to my apartment. While talking on my cell phone, I paid the driver the fare when we arrived at my building, hopped out, and went up in the elevator to my apartment. It wasn't until I was standing inside my apartment that absolute panic set in. I didn't have my BlackBerry, and the last place I had used it was in the cab. Now that cab was barreling down the streets of Manhattan with passengers and toddlers jumping in and out of the backseat, and my vulnerable BlackBerry was going along for the ride—that is, if it hadn't already been kicked out the back door or crushed underneath the seat.

I spent the next three hours in a panic. How many e-mail messages was I missing? What if people were trying to call me and were going into voice mail? Even worse, what if someone had found my BlackBerry and was now looking through my life—e-mails, address book, and the Internet sites I visited most frequently. These thoughts brought an even greater anxiety, and I went into recovery overdrive. I called the Taxi and Limousine Commission to learn about their lost-and-found process, went down to my doorman to see if the cabbie had found the Black-Berry and returned it, and even walked around the block with the slim hope that I would miraculously see the cab and reclaim my connection to the world.

Nothing. My BlackBerry was gone, and there was nothing left for me to do but accept it.

I felt as if someone had taken a cannon and shot a hole in my life. I felt disconnected, isolated, and violated at the same time. I was paralyzed. Unable to spend another waking minute "disconnected," I marched to the nearest store and picked up a new BlackBerry. I walked out of the store feeling as though I had my life back.

My wife—a proud non-BlackBerry user—gave me the sad news. I was a PDA junkie, and my life had been overtaken by a distracting obsession to be connected at all times. I took that BlackBerry on vacation and into restaurants; it rested on my lap during dental visits, was sitting in the bathroom while I was taking a shower, and rested on the nightstand when I went to bed. That little red light blinked wildly in the darkness, beckoning its servant. And while I had that epiphany on my honeymoon, months later I hadn't acted on it. I was a junkie, and I needed to get a grip.

My wife was right, which she is the vast majority of the time. So are millions of other spouses who have similar complaints about their loved ones who had been seduced into digital junkiedom. Several months later, after hearing a familiar-sounding complaint from a friend's husband about her personal digital assistant, I thought about how cluttered my life had become by being "connected" all the time. Yes, it was nice that while skiing in Vail I could still check my e-mails while riding on the chairlift to the top of the mountain, but was that really necessary? Were my messages so urgent that I couldn't wait a few hours until I was back in the lodge to check in with the rest of the world? More important, what did I do before there was a BlackBerry, cell phone, or e-mail?

Following a co-worker's cue—and much to the delight of my wife—I decided to try a "connection holiday." The idea was simple. I'd turn off my PDA and cell phone for a period of time. At first, I started doing it for an hour at a time. My hands were shaking a little, and I was counting down the minutes in my head, but I survived the sixty minutes. When I reconnected—surprise, surprise— the world hadn't blown up. I gained more courage and during the next connection holiday, I extended it to two hours at a time. Then I worked my way over several weeks up to where I could go half a day on the weekends without the BlackBerry or e-mail. I felt liberated. I could survive long periods of time not texting or e-mailing but instead spending quality time with my loved ones and friends, and we were all the better for it. I even felt like I was thinking more clearly.

Taking a digital holiday is a great way to start bringing balance back into your life. Be courageous and be different. Write a letter to someone instead of sending an e-mail. Visit someone and have a conversation in person instead of picking up the phone and sending a text message. Cook a meal for your family instead of ordering takeout. Going back to some of the basics can simplify what has become far too complex and increase the meaningful interactions in your life.

2. The Importance List

When was the last time you really thought about what mattered most to you—not what matters to you and your spouse or companion or kids, but what matters to *you*? What matters doesn't have to be something overly complicated or sophisticated or altruistic. There is no one to sit in judgment to whom you need present your case as to why baking or volunteering at a local shelter or getting your hair done is important to you. It's all about *your* preferences and assignment of importance.

We often get so lost in the hustle and bustle of making it through the day that we don't take time to evaluate which things are meaningful and significant to us and which things are not. Are you spending time doing what matters, or are you filling valuable hours of your day with activities that *others* have deemed important? There is an easy way to figure this out. Sit down in a quiet place without any distractions for at least fifteen minutes and list what matters most. This is creating the Importance List, a list of five items that you can always access and one that will serve as a guide to setting your priorities and will help you get the most out of each day. A sample list (this one is mine) might look something like this:

Spending quality time with the children
Eating at least one meal with the entire
family and not on the go
Doing a good deed for someone
Forty-five minutes of physical activity/
exercise per day
Sending out new photographs of the baby
Reading at least four articles in
a national newspaper
E-mailing friends

Writing in my journal
Cooking a healthy meal
Sending a thank-you card to someone who has
done something nice for me
Going to work and doing my best

Now that you have your list, think about what you've done over the last couple of days. Estimate how much time you spent doing those things on your Importance List and how much time you spent on the things that aren't on the list. At the very least you should aim for an equal split between the two, but ideally as much as three-quarters of your day should be occupied by important things. If you find your level of important activity time is out of whack, then consider reprioritizing and minimizing or eliminating the distractions that are consuming precious hours of your day.

Achieving this balance in your daily regimen will require you to start using the word "no" more often. I admit that for a long time I found it difficult to say "no" myself until I realized the consequences of my always saying "yes." I used to worry that saying no to someone would hurt their feelings, make me appear selfish, or that I would be accused of being a snob. I struggled with this for a long time. I'd say yes to almost any request for giving a speech, attending a function, or helping someone make a social or business connection. Months would pass, and the time would come for me to honor my commitment. I'd invariably begin lamenting the fact that I was going to spend time away from my family or other activities that were more important to me and instead I'd be doing something that I really didn't want to do. I'd beat myself up about it and emphatically announce to my family, friends, and anyone else around that I was simply not going to keep saying yes to everything. I was going to "take my life back." This made me feel better, but it lasted only until the next request rolled in, and once again I was agreeing to yet another appearance without even looking at what was already on my calendar.

3. *Slow Down and Take It In*

Early one morning, at close to 6 o'clock, I was driving along Lake Michigan in Chicago on a road called Lake Shore Drive. It is a popular thoroughfare that connects the north and south sides of the city and provides convenient access to the business districts in the Loop and downtown. Those who know Chicago know to avoid the major expressways during morning rush hour if possible and jump on Lake Shore where traffic is much lighter and the view of the city and Lake Michigan extravagantly scenic. Uncharacteristically, I was in no real rush that morning, so I decided to try something different: drive the posted speed limit. I slid over from the fast lane—the one my car knows very well—and moved into the middle lane. I then slowed down until the needle on my speedometer indicated the 45 miles per hour that was posted on the signs along the road.

The result was immediate. Cars on both sides of me flew by as if I were actually stopped in the middle of the road. Within five minutes of my law-abiding experiment, at least a hundred cars had left me choking in exhaust fumes. Some drivers honked at me; they then swerved to switch lanes and threw up their hands in disgust, even giving me the finger as they passed. How dare I drive the speed limit rather than join the speeding convoy? All of this was at 6 o'clock in the morning when most people were still at home in the middle of a dream.

As I watched the taillights zigzagging in front of me, a thought came to mind: Why were all these people racing so early in the morning to a stress-filled day at work? It wasn't as if they were racing to get to a beach resort for a day of relaxation. Even if they had slowed down just a little, they still would've gotten to their offices and factories on time. But they also would have had the opportunity to appreciate the beauty of the sun dancing across the rolling waves of the lake, the sailboats gliding effortlessly in the soft wind, and the skyline of the city growing against the waking clouds and lifting fog. They were totally missing the calming beauty that could elevate their mood as they headed for another long work day.

We Americans always seem to be operating at full speed, but we also are no longer satisfied with simply focusing on the task at hand. Who isn't multitasking these days? I was stopped at a light recently and glanced at the guy next to me. He was talking on the phone, trying to sip his Starbucks, and fiddling with his BlackBerry. All this while driving. How safe would *you* feel knowing he was headed in your direction? And another guy I saw in the gym the other day was walking on the treadmill with his headphones on, the monitor turned to CNBC, and the *Wall Street Journal* spread across the LCD of his machine. How much of a workout was he really getting?

Simplify your life by slowing down, focusing on the task at hand, and completing it the best you can. As if there weren't enough distractions already, we make it even worse by trying to divide our attention among tasks that require individual attention. Speed might be an advantage when it comes to driving a race car around a track or typing dictation for your boss, but it can be counterproductive when it comes to getting the most out of life and achieving the highest levels of happiness.

4. Release the Golden Handcuffs

When I was in high school, a couple of my friends introduced me to a Catholic priest by the name of Father John. He reminded me a lot of the priest character that Robert De Niro played in the movie *Sleepers*. He dressed like a priest, but he talked and acted like one of us. He didn't use bad language or smoke or do anything against his vows, but there was a coolness about him that allowed us to relax and be ourselves in his presence. We talked about everything from girls to sports to teachers we disliked, and Father John would listen and laugh but never come on too heavy with the preaching. He let us be who we were, and we respected him greatly for that.

One afternoon we went shopping at the local mall. One of my friends worked at a popular sunglass store and would give us really deep discounts on the expensive sunglasses that we otherwise couldn't afford. All of us decided to buy Revo, the hottest brand at the time. We were excited because if we all owned a pair, it would be as if we belonged to our own exclusive club. I waited for Father John to get his pair, but he declined. I didn't understand.

"He's a priest," Matt said. "Priests like him don't have money to spend on sunglasses, even at a big discount."

"Then let's chip in and get them for him," I said.

"It's not just about the money," my other friend Kristian said. "He leads a simple life, and that's what he enjoys."

"But he's always hanging out with us," I said. "He's not like Father Jenson." Father Jenson was another priest at our school. He was rigid, demanding, and went strictly by the book. "Father John likes to have a good time. Won't he feel left out?"

Kristian shook his head. "Don't ask me to explain it, but he's completely happy with what he has," he said. "Seeing other people with nice stuff doesn't tempt him at all. He doesn't need a lot to be happy. That's just who he is. He's simple like that."

How much does materialism distract you from the important things in life? I am thinking about some mothers who spend thousands of dollars to dress their children in name-brand jeans and sweaters, even toddlers who can barely talk and don't know one designer from another. Nor do they care to. They walk around in coats and accessories that would cost the average person weeks' worth of wages. From a very young age we are subconsciously taught the virtues of materialism and designer brands. Wearing a logo confers a status that is instantly recognized and admired by others.

I grew up with little financial means as a child, but

judging by the obsession I had with designer labels, you wouldn't have known it. Every dime I earned from working odd jobs I poured into purchasing anything Izod, the hot brand at the time. Izod epitomized exclusivity and wealth, two characteristics that couldn't be further from the reality of my life. But like any other teenager, I wanted to belong, and that meant owning an Izod sweater or jacket, something that said I, too, could afford the nicer things in life. In many ways I was living a lie. Sure, I could afford to purchase an Izod shirt occasionally, but it took every penny I could save to do so, and certainly the money would have been better spent for something that I needed rather than extraneous clothing that I felt good wearing. The Izod shirts were my version of the golden handcuffs, the hunger for owning the "in" stuff. Common sense said I had no business focusing on things I couldn't afford and whose ownership did nothing to change the reality of my situation.

It is easy to start living beyond your means. The hard part is trying to stop. You become handcuffed to the idea that having more designer jeans or logo-embroidered shirts confers a sense of privilege. This appeals to our desire for others to take notice of us. Does a Gucci handbag really change your life situation and make you happier? Does a Zegna overcoat really make you more special than someone wearing a basic store brand? The advertising for many of these brands would have you believe that just by own-ing these products, you're a "cut above the rest" or "part of the most exclusive club in the world." With millions of dollars spent in marketing these pricey items, it is no wonder that so many people feel they *must* own a partic-ular handbag or drive a limited edition car. We become handcuffed by a materialism that makes us believe our possessions make us better than we really are, and any happiness we derive from this false premise is short-lived at best.

5. Increase Your Me Time

Have you ever sat down and thought about how much of your life isn't really yours? Seriously. That statement might strike you as odd, but let's explore it. One of my favorite features to add when giving a speech is to re-view five things that I believe can instantly improve your health and diet. I go through the right foods to eat, the foods to avoid, reducing fats, and weekly exercise goals. Then I come to number five. But before I get into the specifics of the last task, I ask the audience to think care-fully before answering my next set of questions and then respond honestly with a show of hands.

"How many of you go to work five days a week?"
Every hand in the room goes up.

"How many of you typically work more than eight hours a day?"

Not as many hands as the first question, but close to it.

"How many of you spend some time each day, whether it's a few minutes or an hour, doing something for a family member or friend?"

Same number of hands.

"How many of you spend one hour a day on yourself and not on the kids, spouse, neighbor, or church? How many of you spend that hour doing what *you* want to do for you?"

The silence is immediate, and the hands disappear. Many stare at me with a blank expression; others have a look of embarrassment. The point is made, and everyone understands it. We simply don't spend enough time on ourselves, and most of us don't realize it or fail to do something about it even if we do.

So much of our daily routine is about doing what we *have* to do rather than what we *want* to do. Sometimes the two are the same, but in most situations they are quite different. The list of obligations is endless: take the kids to school, go grocery shopping, pick up the dry cleaning, pay the bills, attend a meeting, reregister the car at the DMV. Most of us could and do fill every waking moment doing things we *need* to do that have very little to do with the things we most *enjoy*. Carving out just an hour each day, a paltry 7 hours in a week of 168 hours, seems to be an arduous task for many.

When I've gotten the audience's attention, I then select a few random people to answer why they can't find a measly hour each day of "me time."

"I'm too busy with the kids."

"I don't have anyone else to help out at home."

"My job exhausts me."

"I don't even know what I'd do with that hour."

I hear that last statement a lot and it always strikes me as the saddest. Not only are we conditioned to fill up our days with activities that aren't meaningful, but if we did step back and live a little for ourselves, we might be lost. Happiness can be derived from the simplest of things: reading a good book, visiting a museum or art gallery, taking a leisurely walk, working in the garden, watching a movie you've been wanting to see, or listening to your favorite music. What you decide to do with the hour is not as important as the fact that you're doing something you want to do. It is your time to be selfish and not worry about what others think. It is amazing how some people can feel guilty spending less than 5 percent of the week on themselves. One thing is certain, if you don't make yourself a priority, no one else is going to do it for you.

Happiness Is a Dead Cell Phone Battery

Who doesn't have a cell phone? Everyone from eight-year-old kids to great-grandparents seems to be speaking into cupped hands or intently staring at tiny screens as they text away. When was the last time you were out in public for 30 minutes and didn't hear a cell phone ring? They are everywhere. Their annoying rings sometimes chirp out the chorus from a popular song or a blaring siren that makes you practically jump out of your skin. No event or place is protected from their discourteous interruption. Weddings, church services, Broadway plays—you name it, and a ringing cell phone has made its unwelcomed presence known.

There's no question that advancing technology has been a benefit to our society's evolution. We can communicate easier, faster, and less expensively than in the past. Along with these benefits, however, come the potential drawbacks: the intrusion of technology in places where we don't want it. Cell phones, while they have made the world a lot safer and more convenient, have also taken away some of the old-school charm of conversations and chipped away at time that used to be reserved for activities that were also about building relationships. We spend less time together because it's so much easier to simply flip open the phone and connect. The intimacy that grew out of friendly visits has been replaced with impersonal text messages that can be sent and received around the clock as well as instantaneous photos that don't need to go to a film shop to be processed.

Given the hectic pace that many of us keep and the bombardment of ringtones, vibrations, and blinking message lights, spending some quiet time away from it all could be good for the soul. Unfortunately, many of us are so addicted to our digital devices that we simply refuse to turn them off when sitting down to a meal or watching a performance. We might switch them to vibrate mode to avoid interrupting others, but we won't turn them off for fear of missing out on something. Whether we want to admit it or not, even in silenced mode we are still thinking about when the next call might come in and who might be on the other end, distracting us from the activity at hand. What is the answer? A dead battery. What we're not able to bring ourselves to do—turn off these pesky contraptions—a dead battery can do for us. Imagine how nice it would be to sit through dinner and have a string of conversations from beginning to end without interruption. Think about sitting on a beach and reading a book with the breeze blowing off the water and the pure sound of the waves without the threat of the piercing shrill of a cell phone. What a revolutionary idea: Happiness can be something as simple as a little quiet time either with loved ones or by yourself when the only thing ringing in your ears are your thoughts or the murmur of good conversation.

YOUR HAPPY PLAN

LEARN HOW TO STREAMLINE YOUR LIFE.

A. EVERY OTHER WEEK DO SOMETHING THAT SIMPLIFIES YOUR LIFE, SUCH AS

- consolidating a credit card;
- converting one of your bills to online bill pay;
- taking back an hour each week and spending it on yourself;
- unsubscribing to an e-mail chain letter or newsletter you get frequently and don't really need.

B. CREATE YOUR IMPORTANCE LIST

- Start with a minimum of five items and keep adding to it until you get to ten.

C. SLOW DOWN

- Every week take a 15–20 minute walk in your neighborhood or a part of town you haven't explored. Take time to observe, learn, and appreciate.

5

North of Zero

✧

Give light and the people will find their way.

—CARL McGEE

Our culture is obsessed with the negative. So much of our country's focus has been on reporting and understanding the negative behaviors and patterns of human beings rather than understanding and accentuating the positive. Walk by a local newsstand and scan the headlines. Infidelity, alcohol and drug addictions, financial embarrassments, a celebrity's fall from grace—we are bombarded with detailed reports of the misery others are suffering. Our popular news that traditionally reported impactful current events has been hijacked by the salacious details of deviant behavior that doesn't contribute anything meaningful to society. And the tabloids can't seem to print enough of these stories because we consume them like ravenous wolves desperate for another morsel of someone else's despair.

This obsession with focusing on the negative goes beyond the gossip mongers and rubberneckers who can't pass by a car accident without slowing down and inspecting the damage (the bloodier and more gruesome the better). The field of psychology hasn't done much better. Psychologists for the most part have been traditionally trained to think about human disease rather than human accomplishment. These scientists approach patients with the question "What's going wrong?" rather than "What's going right?" Counselors and psychoanalysts have been taught that successful treatment means bringing patients from a negative position—let's say minus 10—to even, which would be zero. Here is a graphic representation of how psychology has historically viewed its patients.

Note: The emphasis, as indicated by the size of the condition, has been on studying and helping those who suffer from psychiatric illness rather than spending more time understanding those who are doing well.

Historical Focus of Psychiatry

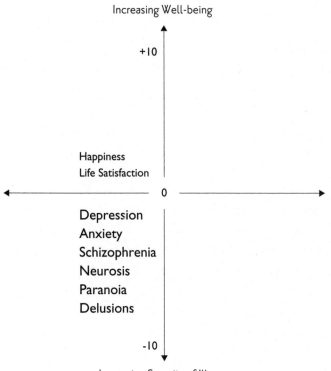

But when positive psychology was founded in 1998, its revolutionary mission was to focus on the positive aspects of human behaviors as they relate to happiness. In other words, analyzing what is going right or taking people "north of zero." This new focus could be graphed like this:

Note: The emphasis has shifted as indicated by the reversal of size given to the condition. The conditions of positive, successful well-being are much larger than the psychiatric illnesses.

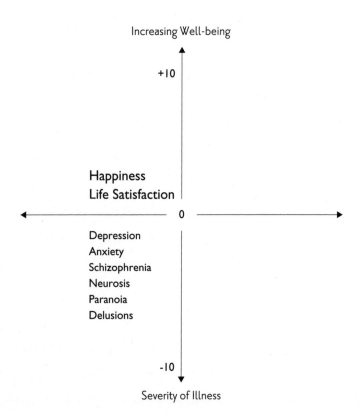

A tremendous amount of encouraging information has poured out of the positive psychology movement. Over the last ten years some of the most acclaimed scientists from all over the world have produced mounds of research analyzing the concept of happiness—what it means and how one can go about achieving it. Unlike other scientific research that tends to be written for those who enjoy esoteric journal articles and complicated textbooks, the findings of this new research are accessible to all of us and can be applied to our lives immediately.

So where do we start if we're trying to go north of zero? Enhancing our interpersonal relationships is as good a place as any. A well-reported 2002 study by famed positive psychologists Ed Diener and Martin Seligman looked at the top 10 percent of students with the highest levels of happiness and the fewest signs of depression.[1] They were asked a series of questions, and researchers learned from their answers that the most significant characteristics shared by these happy people were strong ties to family and friends and a commitment to spending time with them.

Another important study confirmed these results. In 2004, Princeton University professor Daniel Kahneman and his colleagues conducted a large survey that examined how people spent their time, which activities made them happiest, and which activities brought the most negative feelings.[2] At the top of the list of the most positive activities was socializing with friends and family. Again. Other enjoyable activities included relaxing, praying, worshipping, meditating, and eating. Some of the least enjoyable activities included commuting, working, and housework.

Establishing more meaningful relationships with friends, family, and coworkers is certainly an effective way to start going north of zero. Taking on joint projects such as cleaning up a local playground, working together for a charitable cause, carving out time to spend alone and bond, and pursuing common interests are just a few ways to make your relationships more meaningful. Look at some of the marital data. While divorce rates are the highest they have ever been, there is much to be said about those who successfully find the right person and right situation. Research clearly shows that married people are happier, healthier, live longer, are richer per capita, and have more sex than single people. Yes, sex matters. In Professor Kahneman's survey the activity that brought the greatest amount of happiness was intimate relations.

Happiness Means Going for It

Get off the sidelines and get into the game. Life is not a spectator sport. Too many of us are content with the status quo, preferring the comfort of what we know rather than the challenge of discovering the unknown. The happiest people are those with the fewest regrets. It is not because they have succeeded in everything they've tried; rather, they're happier because they at least put forth the effort—win or lose—and tried to make their thoughts and dreams a reality.

Unfortunately, many of us have great dreams and desires, but we're paralyzed by inaction. The fear of failure is one of the biggest reasons for this opportunity-squandering paralysis. Many are afraid or refuse to try something out of their comfort zone because they don't want to face the consequences—embarrassment, feelings of unworthiness, rejection, discouragement—that come with not succeeding. Imagine a young bird deciding to keep her wings clipped by her sides and only walking from place to place. She will be able to cover a considerable amount of ground over the course of her life, but think of all the exciting places and beautiful vistas both high and far she would've seen had she been willing to take the risk and spread her wings to fly. Many humans clip their own wings.

I have always believed that the true spirit of life suggests plunging right in and getting into the mix. Finding your way through life and capitalizing on opportunities means a willingness to throw away fears and to open your mind to the possibilities that populate our path to happiness. For some this penchant for search and discovery might even be genetic. Even as a child I wanted to taste different flavors, try new sports, and take on new challenges. There is something about the unpredictability of an experience that appeals to our human curiosity for adventure. The undeniable truth is that we are not blessed with an infinite amount of time on earth, nor are we guaranteed opportunities. All of us live with personal clocks that, regardless of how great our earthly accomplishments, will eventually come to a stop. Given that we have no way of predicting when our clock will stop, our challenge becomes how to best utilize what limited time we have left.

Many people are more comfortable being risk-averse. They plod through life, staying as much as possible in their comfort zone, satisfied with achieving some level of success and yet readily accepting that they are unlikely to realize their full potential because they aren't willing to take the necessary risks. This group reminds me of the students who are content with just doing the work assigned to them and earning a B. They don't take the chance to do the extra-credit project that could earn them that A. In their way of thinking, why spend all that extra time trying to complete an extra-credit project when it is possible the teacher might not find it worthy and thus not award any points for the extra work. They'll just take the solid, middle-of-the-road B and be satisfied.

There is another group, however, that wants to "live life to the fullest." Its members don't want to play it safe but instead are willing to take risks and are not discouraged that the outcome isn't guaranteed. This group reminds me of my experiences at day camp when I was a little boy. Every day, and sometimes twice a day, we had to go for swimming instructions. The water in the morning was particularly cold, and many of us would stand at the pool's edge reluctantly dipping our toes in the water as we worked up the courage to jump in. There was also a group of campers who would just go for it. They would count to three and dive right in, fully immersing themselves in the chilly water while the others looked on, partly in admiration and partly in dread. It's this group of plungers that are happier in life. When interviewed by researchers, they talk about being driven not by their fear of failure but by their fear of missing an opportunity to maximize life's potential.

Several scientific studies have focused on the connection between happiness and risk-taking behavior. While there is some discussion about which comes first, a willingness to take risks that leads to happiness or a state of happiness and confidence that makes a person more inclined to take risks, there is widespread agreement that a positive relationship exists between risk taking and how happy a person is. A misperception is that happiness is based entirely on the outcome of the action: If you have reached a goal or achieved an accomplishment you've strived for, then you will be happy. But that's not the case. Yes, hitting your mark can be rewarding and give you pleasure, but real happiness is found by engaging in

Taking the Plunge

I. Identify five things you've been wanting to do but have been putting off, such as taking acting classes, asking your boss for a raise, joining an advocacy group such as Mothers Against Drunk Driving, taking a trip to Europe, and so on:

....

....

....

....

....

2. For each of the five things listed above, identify the major reason that you haven't done them.

For example:

Taking acting classes——>
> *Fear of embarrassing myself in front of strangers.*

Asking your boss for a raise——>
> *Worried I'll appear selfish and motivated by money.*

Taking a trip to Europe——>
> *Not enough savings.*

3. Prioritize your list based on the things that you are holding back on versus circumstances you can't control.

As an example, not taking acting classes is something you control and can work on—the fear of embarrassment. This would therefore be at the top of your list. Going to Europe is something you really want to do, but currently your financial position won't let you do it. So this would appear lower on the list.

....

....

....

....

....

4. Once you have established your prioritized list, commit yourself to taking action on one item every two months. If the item is one that is controlled by circumstances, then do what you can to alleviate or change those circumstances. While you might not be able to go on the trip to Europe in six months, at least commit to saving a certain amount each month to build up enough money to go.

the process. Simply going for it can be enough to boost your level of happiness and make you feel good even if your ultimate goal isn't reached.

Every young athlete has heard the expression "It's not whether you win or lose but how you play the game." As a young boy those words didn't mean much to me. I always wanted to win and go home with a Little League baseball trophy. As I got older, however, I realized what Coach Moriarty was really trying to teach us. Playing hard and going for it was the admirable thing to do. If those efforts also brought victory, even better. But if we didn't win the game even after giving it everything we had, we should still hold our heads high. We would know we didn't hold back but gave everything we had out there on the field.

It is useful to step back periodically and ask ourselves whether we are just going through the motions and putting our life on hold for some obscure future promise. If this defines your approach to life's journey, you could be squandering great opportunities that may never come around again. This doesn't mean you should take things to an extreme and suddenly turn from someone who is cautious by nature into a daredevil who skydives and bungee-jumps every weekend. Those are risky behaviors, but they are not the risks we talk about when describing what it means to fully apply yourself and be willing to take on new challenges. Going for it doesn't mean putting your life at risk or unnecessarily taunting danger. Going for it means seizing the moment, taking a chance, and trying to get the most you can out of life.

Happy People Exercise

Beyond its physical and health benefits, exercise can make you happy. Scientists describe two important chemicals that are involved in the positive effects we can get from exercise. The first is cortisol, a hormone that the body produces under stress. When you are angry or anxious or fearful, your adrenal glands produce cortisol to influence changes in the body that will help you adapt and eventually overcome whatever disturbance you are currently experiencing. This is called the fight-or-flight response. But too much cortisol can also be a problem and have negative effects that can ultimately inflame and damage your organs. Exercise burns cortisol, thereby making us healthier and happier.

The second group of chemicals to consider are endorphins. These are often called the body's "natural happy chemicals" because they can decrease the effect of pain and control feelings of stress and frustration: They make you feel good. Have you ever wondered how a soldier who has been injured in battle is still able to continue fighting or save someone else's life? Have you ever thought about what causes "runner's high," that state of pure euphoria some runners experience? Both are largely caused by endorphins that are produced in the brain and can be even more powerful and yield a greater euphoria than opiates such as morphine. Exercise can stimulate the small pituitary gland in the brain to release endorphins, whose effects can be felt even hours after the exercise is over.

There is some debate about which exercises are best to promote happiness, but you should choose exercises that you enjoy and can immerse yourself in without distraction. Vary your workout so that the routine is fresh and your body faces new challenges. However frequently you work out 30 minutes to an hour should be enough per session to get those endorphins flowing and get you feeling good about yourself and what lies ahead.

Act and Think Happy

Happy people think about being happy. In other words, you are what you think you are. This sounds simplistic, but many people don't actually spend any time thinking about whether they are happy or what makes them happy. Your most active thoughts are the ones that will dominate your actions. If you are preoccupied with thoughts of making money, then it is likely you will be driven toward activities (job searches, improving your resume, meeting posted requirements) that will help you accomplish this goal. If you are preoccupied with food, then it is likely you will be driven toward activities where food is a central component (watching food programs, grocery shopping, cooking, eating). If you think about happiness, then you're likely to adopt behaviors and make decisions that will facilitate your becoming happier.

Surprisingly, even pretending you're happy—smiling, mimicking energy and enthusiasm—can not only earn you some of the benefits of happiness but can actually *make* you happier. These are the findings of Sonja Lyubomirsky, a research scientist from the University of California–Riverside, who has devoted her career to studying happiness.[3] Lyubormirsky goes on to explain that there are two feedback loops that matter, one internal and one external. Internally, when we smile, or display happiness in our tone of voice or posture, our brain interprets the physical representations of happiness as the emotion itself; thus we experience the emotion as even greater than it is. Externally, when we display signs of happiness, these manifestations are typically mirrored by others, and this can create a cycle of positive emotions. If you smile and speak in a friendly tone, it is likely that others will respond in kind. Typically, we behave the way we feel: If you are angry, you will scream and throw things in frustration. But sometimes we can feel the way we behave; if you're walking peacefully along the beach enjoying a soft wind and the soothing sound of the waves, it is easier to feel calm and relaxed.

Happiness Is Contagious

You are who your friends are when it comes to happiness. This was the finding of a recent study conducted by researchers at Harvard University and the University of California–San Diego.[4] According to one of the authors, James Fowler, it has been known for a long time that there is a direct relationship between one person's happiness and another's. But this study went even further and showed that happiness can be spread indirectly as well. Not only does your friends' happiness affect your happiness, but there is also a positive relationship between your friends' friends' happiness. This means that, just like a virus, happiness can spread through social networks, and your mood could influence the happiness of someone you've never even met.

The happiness of more than 4,700 participants in the study was measured over a twenty-year period using a standard test for assessing happiness. People were asked to report how often they experienced certain feelings during the previous week: "I felt hopeful about the future," "I was happy," "I enjoyed life," and "I felt that I was just as good as other people."

Then each person's social network was carefully recreated through a computerized program. Connections were first drawn between parents, spouses, siblings, and children. Then information was gathered about "close friends," place of residence, and place of work. The names of neighbors and coworkers, as well as births, deaths, marriages, and divorces, were also recorded. All of these social ties were used to create one big map of connectedness that was combined with the information about each subject's measured happiness.

As you might imagine, the closer the social contact, the greater the chance of happiness being spread. The happiness of an immediate or first-degree social contact increased a person's chances of becoming happy by 15 percent. The happiness of a second-degree contact (such as friend of a sibling) increases the likeliness of becoming happy by 10 percent. The happiness of a third-degree contact (friend of a friend of a friend) increases the likeliness of becoming happy by 6 percent. And that is where the association stopped. No significant spread of happiness was seen in fourth-degree contacts.

This study's finding immediately raised many eyebrows, especially from those who have made a career of studying happiness. But this wasn't the first time these researchers had published this "contagious phenomenon." A little more than a year earlier they found that obesity can spread via social connections, especially when it came to close friendships. The thinking behind this study was that there is a tendency of people who become obese to influence the behavior of those close to them as they convey either overtly or subliminally that it's all right to be overweight. And the friends didn't have to see each other frequently or even live in the same city to have this effect. Friends who were hundreds of miles away had just as much impact on a person's weight as those who were geographically close.

You will not be able to spend the rest of your life avoiding unhappy people, but it might be a good idea to spend your time with those who have a cheerful disposition and are upbeat about life. Happy people are doing something right, so by surrounding yourself with these people who "get it" means an increased chance that good things will happen to you, too.

Happiness Is a Dirty Laundry Room

The longest longitudinal study of adult life ever conducted goes by the unenthusiastic name of *The Study of Adult Development*. Despite the bland name, this research project has provided a wealth of information. Its origins date back to department store magnate and philanthropist William T. Grant of the W. T. Grant Stores who donated money in 1938 to two physicians at Harvard for the purpose of studying healthy development. A group of 268 Harvard students were selected from the classes of 1939 to 1944 to participate in what was conceived as a landmark research project. These 268 men—including future president John F. Kennedy—were initially put through exhaustive medical exams and physical tests, as well as psychological study. They were measured from every angle with almost every scientific tool available at the time. In pre-computer days this information was recorded longhand and added up to a database on everything from physical characteristics to attitude. The data would be used throughout the study to compare with new information that was collected periodically.

The original doctors who started and managed the study have since died, but for the last forty-seven years this treasure trove of information has been under the careful supervision of Dr. George Vaillant, a Harvard psychiatrist who continues to record information on these still anonymous subjects who, if still alive, are climbing well into old age. One aspect of these men's lives that Vaillant has been studying closely is the basis and strategies for finding happiness. In an interview with the *Atlantic*, Dr. Vaillant talked about the happiness he found in the study.

> My image of real happiness in the Grant study is a man whose laundry room was just filled with the laundry that came from his children all loving him and being there and bringing their grandchildren who all helped him garden and helped him sail and produced dirty clothes that needed to be cleaned. But he and his wife had the sense of being matriarchs and patriarchs. I mean the take-home lesson is always to enjoy where you are now.[5]

A laundry room full of dirty clothes may not be an enviable sight to whoever has to take the time and effort to clean them all, but when these clothes represent time spent with family enjoying each other and making the most out of life, then having to clean the evidence of these loving bonds becomes a joyful task rather than a chore.

YOUR HAPPY PLAN

A. AT LEAST ONCE A WEEK VISIT OR HAVE AN OUTING WITH A FRIEND OR GROUP OF FRIENDS. BUDGET YOUR TIME SO THAT YOU CAN WORK YOUR WAY UP TO ENJOYING YOUR FRIENDS THREE TIMES A WEEK.

B. AT LEAST ONCE A MONTH HELP SOMEONE, SUCH AS PICKING UP GROCERIES FOR SOMEONE WHO IS HOMEBOUND, DRIVING SOMEONE TO A MEDICAL APPOINTMENT, OR VOLUNTEERING AT A BOYS AND GIRLS CLUB.

C. SPEAK TO THREE STRANGERS EVERY WEEK. THIS DOESN'T HAVE TO BE AN EXTENDED CONVERSATION BUT SIMPLY SMILING AND ASKING SOMEONE HOW THEY'RE DOING, ESPECIALLY SOMEONE WHO LEAST EXPECTS IT. IT CAN MAKE A DIFFERENCE.

6

The Art of Dreams

✧

Go confidently in the direction of your dreams!
Live the life you imagined.

—HENRY DAVID THOREAU

Dreams are the powerful creations of our imagination. They
sustain us during times of difficulty and inspire us when we
become too complacent. Dreams are the result of imagination
trampling over boundaries. Dreaming makes people happy.
Dreams free us and dare us at the same time, informing us of

the greatness of our individual potential if we are willing to take a chance and venture into the vastness of an alternative universe.

I learned about the power of dreams at a young age when my small family didn't have much money or the creature comforts that my classmates and their friends seemed to have in great abundance. My grandfather was acutely aware that our lack of material status had an effect on me, as it would any young boy who wanted to have the same name-brand sneakers and toys that the other children had. His way of encouraging me to look beyond my present circumstances and remain cheerful was by retelling his own difficult family circumstances: being raised painfully poor in a small North Carolina town. He made the stories of his large family's struggle come to life, emphasizing how much effort it often took just to have a meal on the table at the end of the day. My grandfather had never gotten past the sixth grade, because he had to go to work early in life to help feed and clothe his family.

It was the story of one of his older brothers, Charles, a story that he liked to tell over and over again, that taught me the power of imagination.

"Did you know that your great-uncle Charles traveled all over the world when he was a boy?" my grandfather would say. "You name the country, and he's been there."

"How could he do that?" I'd ask. "You guys barely had enough money to eat. How did he have enough to travel the world?"

Pops would flash that smile full of strong white teeth.

"Not only did he travel the entire world, but he never left the front of our house," Pops said.

He would pause for a beat to set up his punch line and enhance the drama.

"He did it in books, boy. He read everything he could get his hands on and traveled to all those foreign countries in his books and never left our front stoop. The mind is a powerful thing, and it can take you places that your body can't go."

I never got tired of that story or its message, and my grandfather never got tired of telling it. I always walked away from that story inspired by the transcendent powers of our imagination and its magical ability to transport us beyond any current predicament. Regardless of how poor we were or how disconnected we felt, we could mentally lift ourselves and go wherever we wanted and do whatever we wanted.

Examples of our imagination at work are plentiful and instructive. Whether it was a Holocaust survivor talking about how he survived the inhumane agony of a concentration camp or an African woman retelling the torture she endured before escaping murderous gang members, these heroes invariably talked about their ability to stretch their dreams beyond physical limitations and imagine better conditions, happier times, and an end to their suffering. Many of these people overcome the pain of the present by imagining the promise of tomorrow.

The happiest people are fearless dreamers. They use their

imaginations to create hope and possibility. I found an example of the power of imagination in an odd place: by studying people who play the lottery consistently despite never having won. Lottery players will tell you that regardless of how many millions of tickets have been sold to others, there is always a chance that they hold the winning ticket. They are undeterred by the nearly impossible odds. They are optimists whose optimism has been taken to even greater heights with the phenomena known as Mega Millions and Powerball, big jackpot games with unimaginable financial prizes for the lucky winner(s). The multistate jackpot lotteries have created quite a craze, and the enormous size of the potential payday lures even those who don't usually play or who don't believe in the lottery to take a chance at the big score.

One day I overheard a telephone conversation that a friend of mine was having with her sister. Here is the sentence that caught my attention: "I'd give ten million to Mommy and Daddy right off the top." I stopped and without any shame listened to the rest of the phone call as my friend spent close to $200 million in less than twenty seconds. Her sister's spending was equally efficient, and the two of them even had a friendly disagreement over the way they would divide the money between family and friends. It was a rather entertaining back-and-forth full of gated mansions, multi-million-dollar trust funds, maids, private chefs, and all kinds of extravagances that one sees only on TV programs about the rich and famous.

When their conversation was over, I asked her, "What money were you two spending?"

"Mega Millions," she said. "It's rolled over to more than $200 million, and I plan on winning it."

I couldn't help but laugh. First, this rather conservative, straightforward woman who rarely gave in to these types of whims was talking about Mega Millions. Second, she really had a strong tone of conviction that she was going to buy the winning ticket. "Your odds of winning are something like one in 195 million," I said. "You have a better chance of being struck by lightning. *Twice.*"

"I know how bad the odds are." She shrugged. "But the fun is pretending you've won and spending the money in your head. Just imagining all the things I could do with that money to help my family and friends can be a head rush."

While one oft-quoted study showed that lottery winners, regardless of how much they win, typically return to their pre-winning level of happiness within five years, it was my friend's last comment that really caught my attention. What a powerful concept: Just the act of imagining an outcome could be enough to alter one's mood. What if this were applied to other aspects of life? You could do whatever you want and be whatever you want in the privacy of your own mind. And going one step further, what if this could be used to boost your mood? It sure seemed to boost my friend's that day.

Living Versus Surviving

My grandfather often said that sometimes you can be too close to the trees to see the forest. You have to back up or remove yourself from a situation to get a bigger and clearer view of what's going on. That is exactly what happened when, after living in New York City for more than a decade, a friend of mine moved to a much smaller Midwestern town and settled down for a quieter life. We had quite the bachelor life when he lived in New York—going to parties that lasted into the early morning hours, high-brow receptions at museums, Yankee games in the middle of another pennant chase, dinners at world-class restaurants as well as dive bars known for making the city's best burgers. We really lived it up—or did we?

About a year after he had moved, my friend came back to New York City for a business meeting. We met for dinner at one of our favorite steak houses on the East Side. Only a year had passed, but I could already see the difference in his demeanor and the way he expressed himself. He was more relaxed, more reflective, and not obsessed with finding the hottest party or the coolest bar. In the midst of talking about his new, easier life, he said something that really caught my attention. "I feel like I'm living," he said. "I can afford things without breaking the bank. I can drive almost anywhere and not have to worry about ridiculously long traffic jams. I can go to the lake or park and not have to fight with a million other people for someplace to lay out my towel."

Then I, too, left the city for an extended period of time, and all the things my friend had said to me that really didn't register at the time now made complete sense. It wasn't that I loved the city any less or didn't respect its greatness, but after spending some time away, I had a better perspective of the kind of lives we New Yorkers actually led. While most of us thought we were living it up, the harsh reality is that we weren't really living at all. We were *surviving*. It was like the rodeo bull riding competitions where the rider is holding on with one hand as he's being bucked backward, forward, and sideways, barely hanging on. Sure, you can say that technically he is riding the bull, but it certainly isn't the most pleasant of rides. Sometimes it is more like the bull is riding him while he is just trying to survive.

The stresses and inconveniences of New York City living as well as the outrageous costs for even the most basic items—a gallon of milk for more than $6.00—has many of us not only living from paycheck to paycheck and not saving money but making all kinds of sacrifices so that we can maintain our desirable Manhattan addresses. Whether it is heading down to the subway in rush hour and elbowing our way to the edge of the platform to snatch an empty seat in a crowded car or standing in a movie theater line for over an hour to get tickets before they sell out, living in New York is one anxious moment after the other. It is like riding a merry-go-round that never stops, and you can't get off. Your life becomes consumed by strategizing—figuring out the best time to leave work to catch a cab, knowing which end of the train will have the fewest passengers, and deciding which cross streets at what time of the day will have the least amount of traffic as you're trying to go from the East Side to the West Side. Your existence becomes one long series of calculations and gambles where more of your time is spent trying to plan and get to an activity than actually participating in the event you have worked so hard to attend.

Truly living and taking advantage of your environment and opportunities is very different from simply being present and surviving to see another day. It is wise for you to periodically catch yourself, step back, and decide which category you fall in—living or surviving. Then make the necessary adjustments so that you *get* the most out of your efforts rather than your efforts *taking* the most out of you.

Happy People Imagine Creatively

The following is one of my favorite stories I heard someone recite at a medical conference I attended. Read it to see why. It is about two strangers who shared a hospital room. Rajit Arwat had been hospitalized for several months due to his failing kidneys. A longtime sufferer of diabetes, he had received so much damage to his kidneys that he was on dialysis and in desperate need of a transplant. But he was very low on the transplant waiting list because of his age and a host of other medical problems.

One afternoon Arwat heard a flurry of activity in the adjacent empty bay. Nurses and the cleaning staff had been in and out of the room for over an hour preparing it for a new arrival. It had been a long time since Arwat had had a roommate, and he was excited to finally have some company. Later that afternoon the arrival of his roommate was punctuated with a series of painful moans. The curtains between the bays were drawn for privacy, and Arwat listened as best he could to what was going on. He learned several important details. His roommate's name was Phillip Casey, and he had just finished almost ten hours of surgery. A car had hit him as he rode his bike early that morning, and he had broken close to fifty bones. Both of his legs were in casts up to his waist, and because of a fracture in his spine in the neck region as well as a slipped disc, he was wearing a metal halo that stabilized his neck but didn't allow him to turn from side to side. The pain medication was obviously wearing off from the surgery because Casey was constantly asking for more. Arwat could tell that his new roommate was exceedingly uncomfortable.

It took weeks for the two men to develop a rapport. It was slow going at first, mostly because Casey's pain left him complaining to the doctors or ringing the call button for medication that eventually rendered him quiet and drowsy. But as

Casey's injuries began to heal, so did his mood and his willingness to talk to his roommate.

Arwat's bed was positioned next to the wall with the room's only window. Casey's bed was near the door. Given Casey's movement restrictions and the positioning of his bed, he was unable to see out the window. Casey was an avid outdoorsman, so every day and sometimes twice a day he would ask Arwat to describe what he saw out the window.

"Sheer wonder," Arwat would say. "It's amazing how God could make simple things appear so beautiful."

Arwat would go on to describe the sun rising and the way it formed a halo around the trees. He would describe the nimbus clouds as they floated against the pale blue sky as if they had been suspended on invisible cords. Casey's favorite was the sunset. Arwat was an artist the way he described the sun's slow descent toward the horizon and how its positioning affected the color of the autumnal foliage of the trees with robust crimsons and burning oranges. The colorful reflection in the nearby pond was the stuff of postcards. Every once in a while a bird would land just outside the window, and Arwat would describe every detail, from the length of its beak to the vast array of colors that painted its feathers. Casey couldn't get enough of Arwat's intimate descriptions. They were so rich and colorful that he felt as though he was seeing them with his own eyes.

Late one night Casey was awakened by a machine's alarm. A loud chorus of irregular beeps and bells mixed with the commotion of activity. Medical personnel who were dragging machines, wires, and carts were rushing to Arwat's bed. The doctors and nurses were talking to each other in loud panicked voices, and while Casey couldn't understand the medical jargon, he knew something was terribly wrong. He heard one of the doctors call for the defibrillator, and then moments later he was telling everyone to step back. The room fell eerily silent except for the sound of electricity being transmitted from the pads to Arwat's chest. There was a short pause, and then Arwat's body landed heavily on the bed with a thud. Casey, normally not a religious man, started mouthing the Lord's prayer in hopes that his roommate would be saved.

The excitement went on for what felt like hours but was actually no more than 30 minutes. Then Casey heard the same doctor's voice that had been giving instructions throughout the chaos say, "Call it. Time?"

A nurse announced the time.

Rajit Arwat was dead.

Hours later Casey heard the zipping of the bag and, still unable to move his neck, just caught a glimpse of two men wheeling Arwat's lifeless body out of the room. Once they closed the door, Casey spent the rest of the night crying until he fell asleep. He couldn't understand how his roommate, who earlier that day had seemed in the same good condition he had always been in, could suddenly take a turn and die. None of it made any sense.

The next day Casey asked the morning nurse what had happened, and she explained that Arwat's failing kidneys had finally taken a toll, and his heart slipped into an abnormal rhythm that eventually killed him. They did all they could to save him, but it was too late. She, too, was going to miss the friendly man who loved to regale her with funny stories from his native India.

Casey's injuries healed faster than the doctors had expected. New bone growth had filled the fractures in his neck, and a month later the doctors were ready to remove the restrictive metal halo and replace it with a soft neck collar. This was such a relief since Casey could now move his neck slightly from side to side and finally see more than what was in his direct line of sight. They even replaced the special bed he had been using with one that was standard issue. He was excited to move closer to the window where he could now see the great vistas and wildlife that Arwat had described so brilliantly.

Once Casey had gotten settled in his new bed with his body angled just so, he looked out the window. His sharp intake of breath stopped the beat of his heart.

"When did I get moved?" he asked the nurse.

"What are you talking about?" Nurse Brenda Duncan said. She was his favorite nurse, a short fireplug of a woman with a small afro, wine-red eyeglasses, and the scent of honeyglazed apples.

"This isn't my room," he said. "Did someone move me in the middle of the night?"

"Are you feeling okay, Mr. Casey?" Nurse Duncan said, stopping her work with the IV pole and planting her hands on sturdy hips. "This is the same room you've been in for the last month."

Casey looked out the window in horror and disbelief. His only view was that of a brick wall covered with vines.

"Where's the pond?" he asked. "What about all the trees with the leaves changing color and the birds that rest on the windowsill?"

"Pond?" Nurse Duncan said. "Trees and birds? What in the world are you talking about? This room is in the back of the hospital, next to the alley. What you're looking at is the bottom level of the employee parking garage."

"That's not possible," Casey protested. "Arwat saw the most beautiful things—the sun setting, leaves turning colors, ducks gliding across the still water. He described everything to me as if it were a movie."

Nurse Duncan walked around to the head of the bed and rested her hand softly on Casey's shoulder. "I'm sorry, Mr. Casey," she said. "But Mr. A. worked here for twenty-seven years. He was an attendant in that garage, so he knew very well what he was looking at. Mr. A. was a sweet old man. He was always trying to get others to see the better side of life."

Meaningful Ways to
Spend Time with Others

Volunteer together for a good cause.

Learn together by visiting landmarks, museums, or a cultural dance class.

Participate in a project that builds something such as a house for the less fortunate or a playground for a needy neighborhood.

Explore the natural environment by taking a hike or a nature walk or camping.

Make holidays a time for family and friends to reunite.

Listen to an audio book together.

Combine your creative talents—planting a garden, developing an art project, or putting on a play for the community.

Trace and build your family tree.

Spend a day every month making sandwiches and then driving around and giving them to the homeless.

Invite friends over for movie or TV night where you have dinner and watch a popular TV show or movie.

Start a book club.

Pursuing Passion

Passions are the pursuits that make us happy in life. Passions involve the happiness trifecta: meaning, engagement, and pleasure. Passions are unique in the sense that you alone decide what they are. Passions resonate to the depths of our soul and give us reason to be optimistic when things aren't going so well. No amount of nagging from an overly concerned parent or well-intentioned spouse can make your heart love what it doesn't love. Several happiness studies have found that pursuing one's passion is certainly high on the list of what makes people happy.

Our passions are often in conflict with practicality, and it is the resolution of this conflict that presents the greatest challenge. I was recently talking to a relative who was extremely disappointed by a job search. She had been laid off unexpectedly from her job of thirty years and had spent the last five years tearing herself apart with blame. At the same time she tried to get back on her feet and into the job market. She was a hard worker, a quick learner, and open to do almost anything that would get her out of the house every day and return some of the meaning in her life that she felt she had lost with the old job. But there were several things standing in her way, and the most glaring was her age; she was sixty-five years old, the age at which most people are retiring, not trying to build new careers.

After two years of an exhaustive and disappointing search, she asked me how some of these companies to which she had submitted applications could turn her down for jobs that she was more than qualified to perform. The rejection that stung the most was when a local hospital wouldn't even hire her as a patient transporter, the least skilled of all the jobs she had applied for. I broke the sad truth to her that while she had the energy and appearance of someone fifteen years younger, prospective employers were figuring out her age from her graduation date and placing her application in the reject pile for no reason other than they thought she was too old. I suggested that she realign her priorities.

"What are your passions?" I asked her.

"I love to fish on the open water," she said, "especially early in the morning when they're really biting. If I could go fishing every day, I would."

"What about relationships with people you love?" I asked. "Don't you want to spend time with your three grandchildren?" Her grandchildren were all under the age of three, and I knew that she had been waiting a long time to play the role of the doting grandmother.

"Of course I want to spend more time with them," she said. "I want to be a bigger part of their lives."

"You say this, but at the same time you're looking for a full-time job."

"I need the money," she replied.

"Something's not going to work," I said. "You can't spend time pursuing your passions and being with your grandchildren and still work forty hours a week with limited vacation time."

I could hear her thinking through the silence.

"Fishing costs money," she said.

"I know it does. But you could have that money if you lived within your means and stopped placing importance on things that don't bring you real happiness. You live alone in a five-thousand-square-foot house on four acres of land. Do you really need all of that at your age?"

I could hear her sigh.

"Need?" she said. "I guess not. I could be just as happy with less."

"And you could cut your expenses tremendously," I said. "Then you wouldn't have to worry about finding a job to pay the bills. You could move your passions to the top of your priority list and forget about this depressing job search that is only causing you to suffer low self-esteem."

"But I like working, too," she said. "It's important to me."

"Is it as important as your grandchildren and fishing?"

"Not even close."

It is easy for us to get lost in the routine of doing what we need to do to get by. But if we don't draw a line at some point and become determined that our life passions are no longer going to take a backseat, then we can easily spend the rest of our life engaged in routine, unfulfilling activities. At the end of the day these mundane tasks aren't bringing us joy but are only allowing us to check off another item on our to-do list.

A. The Magic Wand. Imagine you have a magic wand. List three situations or things you would make happen if you had magical powers.

1. ....

2. ....

3. ....

B. Create. Every week create something. Whether it is a poem, a piece of furniture, an arts and craft project, or a montage of family photos, use your creative skills in a dedicated project at least once a week.

C. Identify three of your passions and commit at least an hour each week to each of them.

1. ....

2. ....

3. ....

7

Happy at Work

✧

The secret of joy in work is contained in one word—excellence.
To know how to do something well is to enjoy it.

—PEARL S. BUCK

Maybe you read the title of this chapter and laughed. The mere concept of one's finding happiness at work is for some a pipe dream or, at worst, a cruel reminder of how unhappy many of us really are in the workplace. According to a recent Gallup survey, not even half of working adults are completely satisfied with their jobs.[1] The large chunk of time that occupies most of our day's productive hours is precisely where the vast majority of us have an opportunity to become happier and see a significant impact in the overall quality of our life.

Many of my friends who either live in Europe or travel abroad frequently constantly tell me why America has it all wrong when it comes to work. The best way it has ever been put to me is this:

Americans live to work, while we work to live.

There is a lot buried in that statement. We are taught since childhood that a good work ethic is a great American attribute. We built this country through protest and hard work. Using our hands and primitive tools, we transformed this vast wilderness into one of the most productive industrialized countries in the world—and we did it in near record time, especially when you consider how much longer it took the other industrialized nations to make their transformation. Although it is becoming less common, not so long ago most people worked at the same job for thirty or more years, sticking it out until they qualified for retirement. My grandfather worked at the local light and power company, shoveling snow and cleaning offices, for thirty-five backbreaking years before finally retiring. Two of my great-aunts worked at their respective factories for thirty-one years before calling it quits well past retirement age. Their stories of decades of loyal service were nothing unusual. This is the way we were supposed to work in America.

But somewhere along the way work no longer became a means to an end, but rather the end itself. We started to become defined more by our jobs and less by the hobbies we enjoyed or our family's character or our efforts at good community service. Many people worked because that is what they knew best. Millions who had reached retirement age continued working well into their senior years because that was their way of life. And, besides, what else were they going to do with all that free time? Sit around and wait to die?

The Contagious Behavior of Negativity

One of the greatest threats to workplace happiness is the viral infection of negativity. It is often very difficult to detect. It spreads quietly and festers for some time before it starts causing harm. It is critical that you have a heightened awareness when coworkers and/or situations are coated with useless negativity. This doesn't mean that every second of every day at work you're going to be smiling and skipping down the halls. That, of course, is unrealistic. But you have to exert some degree of constructive effort to make sure that you surround yourself as much as possible with positive karma—a distinctive aura, atmosphere, or feeling.

At some job sites you can feel the tension as soon as you arrive on the premises. Whether it is management at odds with employees or anxiety over an imminent round of layoffs, the air of negativity is thick and stifling. You are not a universal problem solver who can simply walk into a situation and miraculously make things better, but if there is an unobtrusive way that you can help defuse the situation, then you should make an effort without overstepping. Peace in the workplace, even someone else's peace, has an impact on your happiness and should be everyone's responsibility from the lowest employee on the totem pole to the CEO. Whether you like your coworkers or not, you spend almost a third of your day with them, and they begin to take on the dynamics of a second family. As at home, if one family member is upset or in a bad mood, there is a good chance that the rest of the household will in some way be affected also.

"Trouble likes company," my grandmother always said. As I've gotten older and collected more life experiences, I'm convinced more than ever of the wisdom of those words. Unfortunately, part of being successful and happy at work means understanding the politics within your department or division and becoming skilled at avoiding situations that will lead to a negative outcome. All of us have worked with an office gossip or rabble-rouser, someone who is constantly mired in controversy and focused on viewing things through the lens of negativity. These people specialize in complaints, whether it's their wages, worksite conditions, too little vacation, or unsympathetic management. They seem to have an infinite number of grievances. While you might agree and identify with some of these complaints, you would do best to avoid involvement because it will eventually drain you of positive energy. Spend your time focusing on what is going well and work constructively to make things better through consensus and collaboration rather than agitation.

Does it matter that we find some level of happiness at work? Absolutely. First take a look at the time commitment. The average person with a full-time job works at least forty hours per week and in many cases even more. That means between Monday and Friday many of us spend at least one-third of our day at work. Except for those who work the night or graveyard shift, this typically means that during the most productive time of the day when the sun is likely to be out and local attractions such as museums are likely to be open, we are tethered to our desks or the cash register or the factory assembly line. Why would people want to spend one-third or more of their day being unhappy and working at a job they don't enjoy doing? Let's look at it another way. If the traditional daily breakdown is nine hours spent between working and commuting, one at recreation, and eight sleeping, that means there are fifteen "awake hours" per day. As many as half of those awake hours are spent working. Most of us therefore spend almost half of our awake time and maybe more during the work week away from our families, friends, pets, homes, and hobbies. It is unfortunate enough that we lose this time with the people and things we love most, but it is even more regrettable when this lost time is also unpleasant.

The other reason it is important to be happy at work is productivity. Researchers such as Thomas Wright from Kansas State University have repeatedly shown that happier workers deliver more product, exhibit other positive work behaviors, are more likely to have fulfilling and positive relationships, enjoy robust health and thus a better attendance record, and tend to get better performance evaluations along with higher pay. Some research has shown that only a 1 percent positive increase in a worker's relationship with the boss is equal to a 30 percent increase in salary.[2] Many managers and corporate leadership have heard and read enough about the superior performance of happier workers to make "happy disposition" a quality they look for when recruiting new hires.

Many people think that happiness at work is impossible for one of these reasons: They dislike their boss intensely, they're doing a job they don't enjoy, or the stress is overwhelming. But positive psychologists and other researchers have taken a closer look at how one can achieve greater happiness at work. Here are five strategies that could bring you greater joy and allow you to perform better at work.

1. Set Goals

One of the major reasons people are unhappy at work is that they feel as though they're swimming aimlessly in circles in deep water, and they don't know which direction will lead them to land. This can be both frustrating and intimidating. Sometimes your supervisor or manager might set goals for you to accomplish throughout the year. Effective managers communicate these goals clearly and collaboratively. Unfortunately, there are plenty of instances when an employee is doing a job he's been hired to do, but no one has discussed a plan of action with him that includes both short- and long-term goals or ways in which he might grow within the company and find success. If you are a casualty of poor communication, here are steps you can take to improve your situation.

• Talk to your supervisor/manager and explain in a nonconfrontational and nonaccusatory manner that you would be grateful for a face-to-face meeting where you can talk about setting goals as well as charting a plan for you to advance within the company.

• Set your own goals even if management has not helped or has been unresponsive to your requests to help form a personal development plan. Even if these are smaller goals, such as having good attendance, being punctual, or completing your assignments before deadline, having some direction can go a long way in making your work feel more meaningful and more fulfilling. Striving toward these self-assigned goals and meeting them means you are not just another employee punching the clock but are someone with purpose. Purpose—a sense of mission and mission fulfilled—leads to greater happiness. The goals you set for yourself should gradually increase in size, value, and difficulty. Don't start off with the goal of becoming the president of the company. It is not that you can't aim toward leading the company one day as an ultimate goal, but it is not realistic to think that reaching the corner office will happen overnight. Start off with something challenging but attainable and work your way up.

As you move from one goal to the next, try to make those goals more visible to management and your coworkers. Be creative. Think outside the box and try tackling problems that might not be in your job description but are beneficial to the company at large, such as reorganizing files and common areas.

• Whether through the "jobs postings" bulletin board or the human resources department, stay informed of other opportunities that exist at your company and the qualifications that are necessary for the positions you find interesting. Make an effort to gain those qualifications.

Plenty of research has shown that effective communication, especially from management, is key to an employee's happiness. Some managers tend to stay behind a closed office door or always seem too busy for a chat, but you have to be aggressive and make sure you get that one-on-one even if it's only for a few minutes to cover a single small topic. This will let your manager know that you're serious about your job and about succeeding. You might also be kept at the top of the list when management is thinking about making personnel changes. If your manager doesn't communicate with you, be proactive and take the first step. Don't always be that swimmer in the deep water waiting for a miraculous rescue. Sometimes you have to strike out on your own and see if you can make something happen.

2. Have Fun

Who says that working has to be all about business? It's no wonder that those who are working eight or more hours without any fun report being unhappy at work. Having fun doesn't mean that management needs to erect a carnival in the parking lot. Creating an atmosphere in which employees take their work seriously but also squeeze in some fun is the kind of balance that can lead to an overall increase in happiness at work.

Studies show a direct relationship between play and productivity. When employees are having fun, they are more energized. Having fun at least some of the time makes people nicer to be around and more likely to go the extra distance for one another as well as the company. I have experienced this firsthand with a team of people who work with me on The 50 Million Pound Challenge, a free national weight loss initiative that we've been taking around the country since 2007. Our team works extremely long and hard hours and travels extensively, often causing team members to miss family events or shorten vacations. These people go above and beyond their job descriptions as we go from city to city, coast to coast, spreading the message of good health and weight loss. One night at dinner I was speaking to a senior member of the team, and she commented on how impressive it was that the team, despite long and tedious hours, never complained about the time they spent on the job or personal time they sacrificed. Why was that? Her answer was simple: "They're working hard, but they're also having fun."

At our next out-of-town event I was careful to observe how the team interacted and what they did in their few precious moments of downtime. I noticed that when they did have a few minutes away from work, they didn't run and barricade themselves in their hotel rooms. Instead, they made plans to spend even more time together, whether grabbing dinner at a popular restaurant, walking and experiencing some of the city's attractions, or meeting at a bar to sing karaoke. The Challenge trips were long and grueling, but mixing in a little fun whenever possible—without compromising the quality or quantity of our work—was what made everyone happier and excited about the jobs we had to perform.

Get a couple of your coworkers and think of ways that you might be able to have more fun at work or even after hours. Some companies organize lunchtime activities such as bringing in guest speakers or performers. Pull together a softball team and join a league at your local park. Set up office pools for big sporting events such as the NCAA Final Four or the Super Bowl. Form a choir or theatrical club that gives performances around the holidays or at other special times throughout the year. Organize picnics where family members can join in the fun and meet one another. Be creative. The possibilities are endless, and they don't require a tremendous amount of money.

3. Find Something You Like

You might not like all or many aspects of your job, but there must be at least one thing you like more than others. Identify it and focus on it. You might not like the long hours that are required, but maybe you really enjoy the company of a colleague who is working with you. Let's say you're a city clerk who has a long commute to the office. The frustration you feel about the travel could be offset by the pleasure you derive from meeting and interacting with new people throughout the day. If you spend the bulk of your time focusing on the things you don't like, you'll keep yourself immersed in a negative space rather than positive flow.

Identifying anything that will give you some degree of pleasure—even if it's minor—means having something to look forward to although you may not be overly excited about your job. Finding that silver lining can change your perspective of what you consider a totally unpleasant experience. While you might think it takes dramatic changes to make a difference, you can do small things that will make your workplace friendlier and even more enjoyable. Try personalizing your work space, whether it be an office or a cubicle, with sentimental items such as family or pet photographs. Decorate your area in a way that speaks to who you are and the things you like. Put out a jar of candy or mints that people can have when they pass by or come to visit you. Post positive slogans or mementos relevant to the current holiday. Add a flowering plant whose growth you can nourish and enjoy on a daily basis.

4. You Are More Than Your Work

Being a productive and reliable employee is certainly something worthy of praise, and there is absolutely nothing wrong with taking pride in your work. But like anything else in life, there are boundaries that should be formed and respected. Some people take their work too far—literally and figuratively; they bring it home and on vacation and every place in between. Like everything else in life, you must have a bigger perspective when it comes to assigning the level of importance to work, and that means accepting that work is only a slice in the pie of life and not the entire pie.

I once worked for a popular TV station in which employees took pride in claiming they were part of the news division. Competition was fierce in our local market, and we were winning the ratings war for the late evening broadcast. One of the researchers on the planning desk had been working there for at least thirty-five years. Her name was Val, and she was a short, serious-looking woman with bent tortoiseshell eyeglasses, a raspy voice, and a total disregard for fashion. She drank countless cups of coffee, regularly chomped on cigarettes out back with the cameramen, and had a Rolodex thicker than a

Stephen King novel. Val was the classic news hound—full of connections, always looking for the next story, and determined to beat the competition. If a reporter or producer was having a difficult time tracking down a source or story lead, Val was the go-to person. She knew everyone, and if she didn't know someone specifically, she knew someone else who did.

I walked by her desk one day after she had gone home and noticed how absent it was of any personal memorabilia. Stacks of old newspapers, coffee-stained reporter pads, and countless files were strewn across her desk. But where others had hung photographs of family and friends or scenic vacation spots, her cubicle walls were bare. I asked a reporter who had known her for many years about her life outside the newsroom.

"She doesn't have one," he said wistfully. "The news business is her life. We are her family."

"But she must have cousins or nieces or nephews, relatives she spends the holidays with," I said.

He shook his head. "She spends the holidays here," he said. "This job is all that she knows."

A year later, after I had moved to another city, I was catching up with my reporter friend and inquired about Val. I wanted to know if the lifeblood of the newsroom was still giving the competition hell.

"What a sad story," he said. "She was diagnosed with cancer about six months ago and died not too long after."

I left that conversation, in which we had covered a variety of topics, thinking only about Val and her tragic demise. She was such a fixture in the newsroom that it was hard to believe she was gone so fast, but what hit me even harder was the emptiness of her life outside those newsroom walls. Val was her work, and the work was Val. How lonely it must have been to lead such a singular life.

One way to enjoy work is to make sure you're enjoying life. When your job becomes all-consuming, moments and tasks that would typically be exciting and worth looking forward to become mundane and uninspiring. A big part of enjoying work is preserving the freshness of it. If you don't keep some aspects of your job interesting and varied, one day simply blends into the next, and you find yourself merely punching the clock and going through the motions. While work is important and demanding, it must always be balanced with the rest of life's important offerings.

This is also true for those who are currently out of work and searching for a new job. Given the tough economic times and shrinking job market, the competition for the few job opportunities is extremely fierce. This means millions of people are spending many hours a day on their job search. Whether it is polishing the resume, attending seminars, or searching the Internet for opportunities, looking for work has become a full-time job for many. While bills need to be paid and finances stabilized, it is still important to maintain a proper balance. The long and sometimes disappointing hours spent on the job search can fuel depression and anxiety. Keeping perspective and optimism in the face of a difficult job market is critical to maintaining overall happiness.

5. Take a Break

Everyone needs to take a break at some point. Whether you are a security guard or an office manager, you need to have some downtime during the course of the day. The amount of time needed will depend on the type of job and its demands, but it is imperative that you schedule at least three or four fifteen-minute breaks to get away from the daily grind. Some people go to the office, sit down at their desk, and leave it only to attend a meeting or go to the bathroom. They even eat lunch sitting in front of their computer, answering e-mails between bites of a cold sandwich. While this relentless pace might make someone productive in the short-term, many studies have shown that it leads to a high burnout rate and work dissatisfaction. Get up from your desk or away from your machine on the factory floor and try to change your environment completely so that you are getting both a mental and a physical break from the day's routine.

Lunch is an ideal time to take a break. The key, however, is to leave the general vicinity where you work and "break the atmosphere." Even eating outside or taking some time to walk on the grounds or do a quick personal errand can make a big difference. This is a perfect opportunity to clear your head and leave work behind. Many people have even started lunchtime walk clubs, exercising away the day's stress and getting reinvigorated to return to the job with an open mind and a positive attitude. But it's important that the breaks should not involve e-mail or other electronic activities.

I worked with a high-level Fortune 500 executive who was one of the most career-driven persons I had ever met. She was smart, ambitious, and extremely successful at what she did. She worked long, hard hours that often involved tedious meetings and constant travel. One day I called her office to update her on a project we had been working on. Her assistant answered the phone and checked her day's calendar to find when she would have a free five minutes to talk to me. As I listened to the assistant review her schedule, I was horrified by what I heard. It was only 8:30 in the morning, and she was booked solid with meetings until 5:00 that afternoon. When I pushed her to find just a few minutes so that I could squeeze in a few questions, I learned that the reality of her schedule was even worse than I had first thought. Not only had these meetings been booked back-to-back, but many of them were overlapping. She was already late for some meetings before the last one had even ended.

A week later this executive and I were sitting down in an airport lounge, and our conversation drifted away from business to our families and the good things in life. That's when I mentioned her schedule. Although it was *her* calendar, she was honestly surprised to hear from me how often she was overbooked. This breakneck pace was simply the norm for her, and she was accustomed to operating that way. Then I asked her how many times throughout the day she went outside to breathe some fresh air or to walk through the building's atrium and look at the impressive artwork hanging on the walls. A blank expression fell across her face.

"I don't do either," she said. "I've never thought about it."

"Maybe you could try it," I said. "Start by asking your assistant not to book meetings closer than ten minutes from each other. That ten-minute gap is your time. Then make sure she has on your schedule at least fifteen minutes every day—not including lunch—that is free of meetings and phone calls. Take those fifteen minutes and do something completely different and unrelated to work."

It took her a month to implement my suggested changes, but when she finally did, she reported how much she looked forward to those fifteen minutes and even directed her assistant to schedule two of these breaks per day instead of just one. She claimed the pleasant interruption in her schedule gave her a different perspective on her work life and helped reduce the stress that used to build throughout the day.

We often find ourselves so consumed by the task at hand that we lose perspective and take for granted the interesting people and environment that surround us. Occasionally downshifting into a lower gear opens up our mind and gives us an opportunity to explore, to look through a lens we rarely use but that can bring tremendous pleasure.

YOUR
HAPPY
PLAN

A. SET THREE GOALS FOR YOURSELF TO BE ACCOMPLISHED OVER THE NEXT YEAR. MODIFY THESE GOALS WHEN NECESSARY AS THE YEAR PROGRESSES.

....

....

....

B. THINK OF THREE ACTIVITIES THAT WOULD MAKE YOUR WORKPLACE FRIENDLIER AND MORE ENJOYABLE. SHARE THESE WITH YOUR COLLEAGUES AND MANAGEMENT AND SUGGEST THAT OTHERS DO THE SAME.

....

....

....

C. WHILE AT WORK SPEND AT LEAST TWENTY MINUTES EVERY DAY PHYSICALLY AND MENTALLY SEPARATED FROM YOUR JOB.

8

Let It Flow

✧

Happiness comes of the capacity to feel deeply, to enjoy simply,
to think freely, to risk life, to be needed.

—STORM JAMESON

Athletes talk about the times when they play so well that they can't seem to do anything wrong. They are focused, determined, and completely in the moment—an exceptional moment when they're at peak performance. Everything goes their way. They call it "being in the zone." Mihaly Csikszentmihalyi, one of the greatest psychologists of the modern era, studied this phenomenon. He called the concept "flow." He describes it as the mental state of operation achieved when a person is fully engaged in what he or she is doing; it is a feeling of energized focus, full involvement, and success in the process of the activity that is being undertaken. Flow is the "optimal experience." It occurs when one is performing at his very best while immersed in a challenging task that demands intense concentration and commitment.

Researchers have found that those who experience flow frequently are much happier than those who experience it only occasionally. But the happiness you get from the state of flow is different from the happiness of buying a new pair of jeans or watching a good movie. The happiness of flow is deeper and longer lasting. According to Csikszentmihalyi, "It is the full involvement of flow, rather than happiness, that makes for the excellence of life. We can be happy experiencing the passive pleasure of a rested body, warm sunshine, or the contentment of a serene relationship, but this kind of happiness is dependent on favorable external circumstances. The happiness that follows flow is of our own making, and it leads to increasing complexity and growth in consciousness."[1]

You don't have to be an athlete to achieve the state of flow. Gardeners, writers, and painters describe it frequently. We all have the potential to experience it if we meet some of the basic requirements.

1. **Clear goals.** The rules must be easily understood.

2. **Matched challenge and skill level.** You have to be involved in a challenge that is just beneath or equal to your skill level. You can accomplish the task at hand, but it's going to take all you've got to do so. If the challenge level doesn't match your skills, then you need to make adjustments. For example, if the challenge is too easy, you get back to flow by increasing the level of difficulty. If the challenge is too difficult, then you must learn new skills that will help you meet the challenge.

3. **Distorted sense of time.** Time passes, and you don't even notice it. Minutes become hours, and because you're so absorbed, you have no idea how much time has elapsed while you've been in the activity.

4. **Disappearance of the unrelated.** People in flow also have a tendency to be unaware of what's going on around them. Very few if any of your thoughts are related to anything other than the task at hand. It is almost as if the rest of the world dissolves into a quiet background noise that you can't hear and do not care about.

5. **In control.** You are not afraid of being out of control because you know that you can control the situation or activity if necessary.

6. **Effortless.** While the challenge might be difficult, you feel the task at hand is effortless. Succeeding in the activity itself is rewarding and far outweighs the external rewards that might be waiting.

7. **Intense concentration and focus.** You must reach a high degree of concentration on the activity at hand so that you can focus sharply and delve deeply into the task.

8. **Loss of self-consciousness.** Action and awareness merge, and there is no time for self-monitoring and self-criticism.

9. **Direct and immediate feedback.** The instant feedback of your actions' successes and failures while performing the activity are obvious, so behavior and decisions can be adjusted as needed. This is true when playing a game of chess, poker, or tennis as well as other involving activities such as painting, gardening, and playing a piano. A tennis player knows after each shot whether the ball went where he wanted it to go, just as a pianist knows after each strike of a key whether the note sounded the way it should.

Everyone is capable of flow. It is possible that you have already experienced it and didn't even know you'd been in it. My first experience with flow happened when I was eleven years old. Every summer I attended the Green Knoll Day Camp, an adventurous sprawl occupying more than a hundred acres of pristine wooded land. With a lake, horse stables, two swimming pools, and more land than any of us could ever imagine exploring, the camp was an oasis for those of us who loved the outdoors and the endless activities that could fill our day. One such activity was archery. The camp had two ranges, and one of the highlights of the week was a chance to stand before those targets and fire arrows from 60 feet away.

I was an above-average archer, a respectable feat since I had learned it while at camp and practiced it only while at the camp's facilities. Some of the other campers were fortunate enough to have their own high-tech bows and an opportunity to shoot at home with their fathers. One such boy was John Palmeroy, the envy of all of us with his highly glossed wood bow and a bag full of professional accessories that the rest of us didn't even know were part of the sport. Even the camp counselors admired Palmeroy's expensive gear and his practiced ability to strike the target at will. One of Palmeroy's greatest tricks was standing even farther back than the rest of us and still hitting that bull's-eye with a consistency the rest of us could only dream of. I was impressed by his equipment but not daunted. I practiced as hard as I could every chance I got.

The big deal at the camp was the end-of-the-summer archery competition. Our weeks of learning and practice were meant to get us prepared for this important contest. The competition was camp-wide, with each of the age groups—tribes—crowning a champion. But the champion of our tribe—the Mohawks and the oldest of the age groups—was most important because he was crowned the champion archer of the entire camp. Winning was important for more than bragging rights and your name being carved in the camp's legendary plaque of great archers. The camp's champion archer got to shoot the flaming golden arrow into the bonfire on the closing night of camp when all the older children and the parents were in attendance at the ceremony.

It was a foregone conclusion that Palmeroy and his high-powered bow were going to win by a landslide. The rest of us were using camp-owned equipment that was worn-out and couldn't compete with all the expert marksmanship accoutrements attached to Palmeroy's bow. The archery competition was taken very seriously by the entire camp, and we competitors sat in rows in front of the targets, waiting for our turn to shoot. Each round was recorded by the counselors; they carried clipboards and meticulously examined the arrows that struck the target and recorded our scores. During this competition they were sticklers for rules and protocol. We were given only three arrows to shoot per round, and once our round was over, the counselors would go from one target to the next and retrieve the arrows while keeping track of our scores. Sometimes a debate would break out if an arrow seemed to have split the line between two adjoining circles on the target, but for the most part the hit was clear.

I remember that my first round was surprisingly good. I hit two bull's-eyes and a red. It wasn't as if I hadn't done that before, but what really caught my attention was how easy it felt. It was almost effortless—loading the arrow, pulling back the string, and firing. For some reason it felt so smooth and automatic. One of the counselors gave me a nod of approval for my score for that round, and I went to the back of my line and waited for the second round. When it came, I felt the same way. This time, however, I recorded all bull's-eyes. This was something I had never done. My counselor looked at the target and then looked back at me suspiciously. Even he was surprised at my results.

I can remember having an out-of-body feeling. Everything around me except for the bow, arrow, and targets seemed to blur into the background. The other campers were talking and making noise, but I was too focused to hear their conversations. My concentration was strictly limited to the task at hand, and I thought about my form, how I loaded the arrows, and how far back I pulled the string before release. I wanted to duplicate each step so that my coming rounds would also be successful. My sensibilities were greatly heightened. Even when I wasn't holding the bow, I could still feel the smoothness of the fiberglass pressing against the palm of my hand. I could feel the tension of the bow string in the bend of my fingers and the sharpness of the arrow feathers as I prepared to launch. First the snap of the string whirred next to my ear; then there was a loud thud as the arrow pierced the target. I even lost track of time, unsure of how long I was waiting for my next turn or how long it was taking me to complete my shooting round.

Miraculously, I won the archery competition that day by beating Palmeroy, the odds-on favorite. No one wanted to believe it had happened, and even I was struggling to figure out how I had put so many great rounds together. It wasn't as if I had any high expectations going in. I didn't practice the night before (as Palmeroy did), because I didn't have any equipment of my own or a place to practice other than the normal archery class. I didn't even have any thoughts about the competition. I expected it to be simply another activity on the day's agenda. I was hoping to do well enough not to embarrass myself, but actually walking away with the best score had never occurred to me.

I remember feeling some happiness while scoring all those bull's-eyes, but it wasn't the level of happiness you might expect given the tremendous scoring success I was experiencing. It wasn't until that afternoon when the competition was over and I was heading home that I felt the full brunt of happiness. According to the experts, it's to the advantage of the person in flow not to acknowledge happiness during the challenge. It would only serve as a distraction that could potentially throw one off course and lead to failure.

Later that week in the camp's closing ceremony, I stood in front of everyone. One of the counselors lit the end of an arrow until it flamed, and I shot it into the bonfire, which then ignited brilliantly against the black sky. It was one of the happiest experiences of my childhood.

Flow is all about surrendering to the moment. It is the opposite of multitasking, where your efforts and concentration are divided. The single-tasking during flow increases your level of productivity and allows you to reach your goals.

Flow feels so good that it becomes addictive. Golfers will quickly attest to this. In a game that most of the time can be extremely frustrating and unrewarding, millions of people still return to the golf course again and again—even after shooting a miserable score. They come back because they have experienced flow even if it was only on one hole of eighteen, and they want that feeling again. It is the same with artists. They know what flow feels like when the brush seems to guide itself and the results on the canvas are magnificent.

Flow, like life, is all about evolution. What might have brought you to flow as a teenager might not work as an adult. This is not surprising because as we age our performance skills change. Since the challenge must match your skill level for flow to occur, you can imagine that with practice your skills will sharpen and thus the challenge will get more difficult. Think about the young pianist first learning how to play. Simple songs such as "Mary Had a Little Lamb" and "Twinkle, Twinkle Little Star" are reasonably difficult for the beginner. An inexperienced player could achieve flow when finally able to perform these songs flawlessly. But those who have been playing the piano for twenty years have skills that have outgrown such simple arrangements. They likely need something like a Beethoven sonata to be enough of a challenge to match their advanced skill set.

Ironically, many of us get our major flow opportunities while at work. This might seem strange since so many people associate work with stress rather than happiness. In fact, while on the job we tend not to recognize or enjoy these flow opportunities because we are so caught up with the imperative to complete a list of tasks before the workday is over. Pressure from our bosses, deadlines, and coworkers can ruin our opportunity for flow. But imagine how advantageous it would be if you learned how to capture these flow opportunities at work. It could make you feel better about your job and make the time pass more quickly. What would be better than to be so absorbed in your job that you lose track of time, and before you know it, you're on your way home?

Achieving flow at work is possible by following a few key steps.

1. **Focus on Important Tasks.** Not everything you do at work will be important. In fact, it's completely fine to enjoy work that is easy and unimportant. But if you can concentrate your time on the more important tasks, that will have a long-term impact on your life, career, and others around you. You will also be more likely to find flow. Let's say you're an executive assistant. Your major responsibility is supporting your boss and making sure his professional life

is organized and efficient so that he can be more productive. This means that you should be focused on those tasks that deliver these results. Some of these tasks might include keeping a meticulous calendar, creating a clear and comprehensive filing system that is simple but effective, and organizing his travel schedule so that every detail is thought of from the time he leaves his house to the time he returns.

2. **Challenge Yourself to a Point.** Finding the right degree of difficulty in a challenge is critical for finding flow. Always choosing tasks that are too easy will not yield the opportunity to enter flow. It is equally important not to choose tasks that are beyond your skill level because you won't be able to accomplish them regardless of how hard you try. Finding the right balance might take time, but once you get it right, you'll know it. Let's say you work as a stocking clerk in a grocery store. Your job is to line up product on the shelves and account for inventory levels. But you might also take this a step further. Challenge yourself by not just spending hours loading product on shelves but thinking about strategic merchandising. Which products might work best being sold next to one another or in the same aisle. This might be beyond your job description, but it can be a stimulating challenge that keeps you engaged in your job and also attracts the attention of your bosses.

3. **Streamline Your Environment.** Distractions can do just that: distract from our ability to focus on the more important task at hand. Whether it is your cell phone, PDA, or instant messaging—whatever will suddenly blurt out and interrupt you should be turned off. Set your computer's e-mail inbox so that each incoming e-mail isn't announced with an electronic ping. You'll have plenty of time during other parts of the day to tend to these personal communications. Also, make sure your work environment is orderly and not cluttered. If you have a desk, arrange it so that the fewest items are on it. A crowded desk leads to a crowded mind, and this can certainly distract you from more important thoughts.

4. **Choose Work You Enjoy.** If only we could all be professional athletes or movie stars, then we'd always be able to do the job that we love. But the reality is that there are times when we have to take a job that we don't necessarily enjoy because we need the money or we're finding it difficult to find employment in the line of work that we want. There are other times when we actually get a job we enjoy, but there are still parts of the job that are not so favorable. Nevertheless, we must perform those unfavorable tasks as well. If you have the flexibility to choose work that you love, then you're lucky and should be appreciative of your good fortune. Take advantage of that. If you aren't at a job that's 100 percent

satisfying, do your best to choose projects or focus on the parts of the job that are most meaningful to you and bring you the greatest satisfaction. You might work for a marketing department for a large corporation. Your day-to-day responsibilities might be purchasing advertising, but that's not exactly what you want to do. You really want to help analyze and secure potential sponsorship opportunities for your company. Sponsorships are handled by your department, but in a different area. You might be able to talk to your boss and volunteer to help out occasionally on new sponsorships as it relates to buying advertising for the sponsored campaign or event. This is a way to come through the side door, but you can get yourself on a project in the area that you really enjoy. Take this opportunity to work hard and shine.

Pursuing new challenges is essential to our ability to find new opportunities for flow in our life. Refining our skills to meet these challenges is a way of getting meaningfully engaged. Imagine how boring life would be if as we aged the level of our challenges remained the same. Some social scientists believe there is something about human nature that causes us to continually search for personal development through learning new things, inventing new things, and working at refining our skills. Whether it's at work, at play, or in social situations, we have the ability to achieve an optimal experience that will bring us meaningful and lasting happiness.

YOUR HAPPY PLAN

A. List five important tasks and make them your focus.

....

....

....

....

....

B. Think of three challenges that you have thought about but haven't taken up.

....

....

....

C. List three ways you can declutter your life.

....

....

....

9

Happiness Boosters

✧

Success is not the key to happiness. Happiness is the key to success. If you love what you are doing, you will be successful.

—ALBERT SCHWEITZER

Once a grouch, always a grouch. This is not so, say researchers who have investigated whether it's possible for those who are distempered to be able to turn that frown into a smile. While research shows us that 50 percent of our happiness level falls out of our control and is determined by our genes, the good news is the same research shows us that 40 percent is within our own control.[1] This affirms what I had discovered in my own life. Exhibit A—my grandfather.

My grandfather, Pops, was and still is a classic. A product of the deeply segregated South, he grew up poor and uneducated, and was left alone to struggle for a better life. With two sandwiches in a cardboard box and less than $5.00 in his pocket, he boarded a train for the great North where rumors had it that racism wasn't as prevalent and a hardworking man, regardless of the color of his skin or level of education, could earn an honest dollar.

To say my grandfather worked hard all his life is as much of an understatement as saying the Pope practices Catholicism—a strong work ethic was that central to his core being. I remember sharing a bed with him as a little boy, and during those bone-chilling New England winters he would slowly get up from the warmth of the covers and methodically put on his clothes, saying little except "Do well in school today. Stay out of trouble. Keep the red thing [tongue] behind the white thing [teeth]." Translation: Don't talk back to adults. And that was the extent of his morning conversation. There was never an "I love you" or "Can't wait to see you when I get home tonight." He'd tie up those old steel-toed black boots with the cracked leather, slide on his trademark French cap tilted to one side, and then head out into the cold.

Pops was a heavily disciplined man, almost to a fault. He

would never kiss us—because boys don't kiss boys. He cut the grass on the same day every week, shoveled snow off the porch and sidewalk in the same sequence, and prepared the same lunch every morning—two pieces of well-done toast and a thick slab of government cheese. Barrel-chested with powerful arms and sterling white teeth, he was a gruff man full of superstitions and a rigid code of conduct. He only spoke to do one of two things: complain or teach us a lesson, taking equal pleasure in both of them. Oh, and hugs were definitely out, too. Pops didn't hug people. He offered a stiff right hand—"A man always shakes with the right hand"— and a grip that could bend steel. But as gruff as Pops was, he was a great provider and always put his family first. He just struggled when it came to the typical displays of affection. Trying to extract even the slightest physical or verbal confirmation of his love was more difficult than passing kidney stones.

For most of my childhood I thought Pops simply didn't like people. He barely spoke to those who spoke to him, and when he did, four or five words were the most he was willing to say. He was content minding his own business and leaving others alone. He didn't ask for favors so that he wouldn't be indebted to others who might lend a helping hand. He rarely needed to verbalize what he was thinking because the way he could cut his eyes and tighten the muscles in his face told you everything you needed to know.

Then my grandmother died. They had been married for

more than fifty years. It was an old-fashioned marriage: He was the breadwinner; she reared the four children and made sure the home was comfortable and full of love. The only time I ever remember them kissing was at their fiftieth wedding anniversary celebration when the children and grandchildren cajoled Pops until he relented and bent over in front of all of us and pecked my grandmother's cheek. Something shot through me watching him do that, and to this day I can replay it over and over again in my mind in slow motion.

At her death announcement and funeral services, the rest of us were a complete mess, but as you might expect, when it came to Pops, there were very few tears. It wasn't that he didn't love my grandmother or wasn't saddened by her death. Crying just wasn't something he did. Several months later was the first sign. I went to visit him at the house that was once so vibrant and busy and was now empty without my grandmother shuffling around the kitchen or sitting in her favorite seat in the living room.

Everything was arranged exactly the way it had been when she was alive, but now with all of us living in our own houses, Pops was left there alone with nothing but silence and her memories. Then he cracked—not a big one, but enough for me to take notice. He actually told me a joke. Then he laughed. It wasn't a roar that shook the walls, but it was a laugh finished off with a tight smile.

Several months later the most amazing thing that ever

happened between my grandfather and me took place when I was about to leave his house after a Sunday visit. I reached down to hug him, and not only did he let me kiss him, but without my saying it first, he said, "I love you." I was temporarily paralyzed. I knew what I had heard, but I also knew it would be a mistake to make anything of it. So fighting back every urge to make a fuss, I simply returned the gesture and got out of the house as fast as I could before he did something like take it back. When I got into the car and was on my way back to New York City, I called my mother and told her what had happened.

"He's doing things like that lately," she said. "He's been calling us up on the phone, telling funny stories about his childhood, and asking about the next time the family plans to get together."

"I can't believe this," I said. "He's actually getting softer in his old age."

"In all my life I've never seen him like this," my mother confirmed. "He's happier and more engaged. He's like a brand-new person."

Just to be clear, it wasn't as if Pops had turned into the happiest person in the world, where he was bouncing off the walls and writing us love poems, but he had definitely undergone a transformation—a big one for him—from an unhappy, distempered person to someone who was more engaged and appreciative of those around him. He was spending more time with us and openly acknowledging what he was grateful for. He was happier not just in his actions but in his words, doing and saying things I had never heard him say. New research on happiness tells us that even those prone to habitual melancholy and grim temperament can lift their mood through a series of exercises and behaviors that are surprisingly simple and quite easy to accomplish. I have listed some of the most popular of these boosters that could also give you a lift.

Commit Five Acts of Kindness Each Week

How many times did I hear growing up, "When you do for others, you're also doing for yourself." Another stalwart in our home was "It's better to give than to receive." We had been indoctrinated with the belief that selflessness was not only a way to feel better about yourself but was one of the important keys to eternal salvation. Scientists decided to put to the test what Bible-toting grandmothers already knew as truth.

There had been hints in earlier research that individuals who report having a great interest in helping people act in a prosocial manner, or have intentions to perform selfless or courteous behaviors are more likely to rate their disposition as happy. Attempting to build on this earlier work, researchers in one study asked participants to practice random acts of kindness regularly over a ten-week period.[2] The acts included such things as doing a roommate's dishes and holding the door open for a stranger. According to the results, how often the kind acts were performed had no impact on the level of reported happiness, but the variety of the kind of acts did. Those who performed a wide range of kind acts reported increasing happiness even as long as one month after the study was completed. Those who reported their events of the past week rather than focus on acts of kindness showed no changes in their level of happiness.

Then the study went further. Did it matter when these acts of kindness were performed? Students were asked to perform five random acts of kindness each week over a six-week period. These acts had to be done either in a single day or across the week. The acts of kindness were behaviors that benefited others and included visiting a sick relative, donating blood, and dropping coins into a stranger's parking meter. The results were clear: Happiness levels increased, but only for those who performed all their kind acts in a single day. Let's call it the "day of kindness." Researchers speculated that when kind acts were spread throughout the week, the effect of each kind act was dispersed so that participants didn't distinguish between their normal behavior and the kindness prompted by the exercise. Taking both interventions together, happiness can definitely be boosted by intentional acts of kindness, but the impact of feeling good about your deeds depended on the timing and variety of performing such

Examples of Random Acts of Kindness

Make a meal or purchase a meal and give it to a homeless person.

Send flowers to someone in your company who is hardworking but underappreciated.

Visit a nursing home or senior citizen's home and bring a gift for the residents to enjoy.

Donate a winter coat to a family whose children might need one.

Leave an inspirational book on the seat of a bus or train with a note for the finder to enjoy it and pass it along when done.

Cut an inspiring story from a newspaper or magazine and post it on a bulletin board for others to read.

Collect things that might be needed at an animal shelter, such as blankets, toys, cat litter, etc., and deliver them to the shelter.

Run your own canned food drive and donate all the food to a residence of displaced families.

Anonymously send something that you know a friend or loved one needs.

Help a school or church plant a garden.

activities. The group that didn't practice acts of kindness experienced a reduction in happiness over the course of the six-week period.

Why do acts of kindness work? Many believe that they bolster one's self-regard, increase the number of positive social interactions, and enhance charitable feelings toward others—all things previously believed to make people happier. Acts of kindness can inspire others to like you more and have a greater appreciation of your behavior, and potentially they can lead to reciprocal kindness. One of our basic human needs is to feel connected to someone else and establish some type of meaningful relationship. Committing acts of kindness satisfies this need.

Keep a Gratitude Journal

The benefits of gratitude are nothing new to religions and philosophies that have long embraced it as virtuous and an integral component of spiritual and physical well-being. Scientists have come late to the game of trying to understand what if any role gratitude plays in the attainment of happiness. Several studies over the last ten years have been undertaken to discover and better understand this relationship. One landmark study was performed by Dr. Robert A. Emmons of the University of California–Davis.[3] He looked at whether keeping a gratitude journal in which people recorded on a daily basis the things they were grateful for would have any impact on their level of happiness.

Emmons worked with three experimental groups over the course of ten weeks. Those in the first group were asked to list five things they were grateful for that had happened in the last week. This was called the "gratitude condition." The second group was asked to list five daily hassles from the previous week. This was called the "hassles condition." Members of the third group simply listed five events that had occurred in the last week, but they were not told to focus on the positive or negative aspects. This was the "events or control condition."

Some of the things that people in the gratitude condition listed included "waking up in the morning," "the generosity of friends," and "thanks to God for giving me determination." Examples of hassles that were listed included "hard-to-find parking," "messy kitchen no one will clean," "finances depleting quickly," and "doing a favor for friend who didn't appreciate it." The last group listed such things as "talked to a doctor about medical school," "learned CPR," "cleaned out my shoe closet," and "attended Whole Earth Festival."

The gratitude group came out way ahead. They felt better about their lives as a whole, were more optimistic regarding their expectations for the upcoming week, spent significantly more time exercising (nearly 1.5 hours more per week), and reported fewer physical complaints.

Other studies have shown benefits from gratitude. Participants who kept gratitude lists were more likely to make progress toward important personal goals (academic, interpersonal, and health-based) over a two-month period compared to subjects in the other experimental conditions. Those in the gratitude condition were also more likely to report having helped someone with a personal problem or having offered emotional support to another.

Write Someone a Thank-You Letter and Visit

Saying thank you is not just good manners. The process of recording your gratitude on paper and even delivering it yourself to the person to whom you're grateful can go a long way in boosting your happiness. One study asked some of the participants to write and then deliver in person a letter of gratitude to someone who had been especially kind but had never been properly thanked.[4] After doing this for one week, researchers found that participants were happier and less depressed. This result was seen as far out as one month from the date of the gratitude visit. What the researchers are now trying to figure out is whether repeating this on a monthly basis is the best way to achieve happiness for longer periods of time.

Why does showing gratitude work? Noted experts such as Martin Seligman believe that it amplifies good memories about the past and creates strong bonds with someone from your past who is important. Thanking others for good deeds has become so customary that it is more of a reflex than a heartfelt display of appreciation for an act of generosity. By taking the time to really think about why you're grateful, to write a letter of thanks, and to deliver that letter in person, you can feel the real power of appreciation that makes you feel good about acknowledging someone for his or her good deeds.

Gratitude also works by focusing on the good things that happened in the past. If you take the time to think about what you have to be thankful for, then that means there is less time to think about the bad things that happened. Imagine a constant battle between the good and evil forces trying to occupy your thoughts. Only one can dominate at a time. The more time you spend on one, the less time you can spend on the other. By devoting more time to thinking about and expressing gratitude, you allow the good forces to win and all the positive energy that comes with them.

List Three Things That Went Well Today and Why

Too much of our day is focused on the bad things that happen or the things we wanted or expected that didn't happen. This often leads to feelings of disappointment, failure, and negativity. But research performed by a group of psychologists led by Martin Seligman has shown that recognizing the good that happens in your day can boost your levels of happiness.

In this groundbreaking study the researchers asked over four hundred participants to perform happiness interventions over a period of several months.[5] One of these interventions involved listing three things that went well each day and identifying why those three things went well. This was done every night for one week. It was one of two exercises that showed the greatest results, increasing happiness and decreasing depressive symptoms for six months.

The exercise might look something like this:

1. I got accepted into one of my top three college choices. This is great news because I like the campus and curriculum at this college, and the school also offered me a scholarship to help reduce the cost of attending.

2. I read a book to a group of toddlers at the library today. It went so well that the librarian invited me back to read another book.

3. I spoke to a friend I hadn't spoken to for several months because of an argument we had. We talked about the merits of the argument, our different viewpoints, and

how bad we both felt about not speaking to each other. We agreed to put the disagreement behind us and move on with our friendship, which we both enjoy.

Spend Money on Someone Else

Having money might not buy happiness, but *how* you spend it could actually make a difference. This is the premise of a study conducted by a team at Harvard Business School and the University of British Columbia.[6] One of the researchers said that they wanted to test the theory that how people spend their money is at least as important as how much they earn. Participants in the study were asked to rate their general happiness, report their annual income, and detail their monthly spending, including bills, gifts for themselves, gifts for others, and donations to charity.

Surprisingly, they found that regardless of how much income each person made, those who spent money on others reported greater happiness while those who spent more on themselves didn't.

In a different experiment the same researchers focused on the employees of a small Boston company. They surveyed the employees before and after receiving profit-sharing bonuses between $3,000 and $8,000. They found that employees who devoted more of their bonus to pro-social spending experienced greater happiness after collecting the bonus. How an employee

Meaningful Ways to Spend
Money on Others

Purchase a dress or pants and a shirt for a toddler and give it to a family that needs it.

Anonymously donate to a church a holiday gift that will be distributed to the less fortunate.

Purchase lunch for a colleague.

Purchase a toy for a sibling or a child in your community.

Quietly slip $10 (or more if you can afford it) to someone who needs it.

Offer to pay for the groceries of someone who is standing in the checkout line.

Find a charity whose mission you would like to support and donate money.

Purchase several books and donate them to a classroom.

Help pay for the school tuition of someone else's child.

Send a gift basket and words of encouragement to someone who might be having a difficult time.

spent the bonus was a more important predictor of their happiness than the size of the bonus itself.

Strengthen and Deepen Personal Relationships

When it comes to finding happiness, relationships certainly matter, but a casual friendship is not enough to make a difference. A study performed by psychologists Ed Diener and Martin Seligman showed that the happiest people had close friends, strong family relationships, and romantic relationships.[7] Unhappy people spend more time alone and have social relationships that are worse than average.

Research also shows that it is not the *number* of relationships that matter, but the *quality* of the relationships. Friends are a great support system; they help us celebrate the good times and weather the tough times. It has been shown that a strong social network is also associated with lower levels of stress and a longer life span. This network should be the old-fashioned kind rather than one that's virtual on a Web site such as Facebook or MySpace.

Establishing meaningful friendships takes time and work. If you don't currently have a network of friends, you need to get out there and put yourself in a position to meet new people. Everyone you meet isn't going to become a friend, but the more people you encounter, the greater the likelihood that you will find a match. Listen to your gut. Sometimes you can tell right away if someone gives off positive or negative vibes. Don't prejudge people before giving them a chance to speak for themselves; but if you are getting a bad feeling about a person right from the beginning, it is more likely than not that this uneasiness is warranted, and you should proceed with caution.

Meaningful friendships take time. Our lives have gotten progressively busy, and many social opportunities exist, from ballroom dance classes to online chatting or participating in advocacy groups. It is easy to fill up your calendar with many less important things so that there is little time left to spend with those who mean the most to you. This has happened in my own life. I recognized it recently and decided to change. My best friend from college has been like a brother to me for many years. We stayed together over the summer, traveled to each other's homes throughout the year, and spoke either in person or on the phone almost every day. Then life happened: marriage, kids, jobs. Our communication diminished drastically, and we were seeing each other only once or twice a year. I brought this to his attention recently, and we both lamented how life's routine had squeezed out many of the things that mattered most to us, such as our spending time together and enjoying the special bond we shared. We agreed on the spot that at least once a year we would take a trip together—just the two of us, no families involved. Whether it would be hiking the Rockies, sitting on a beach in California, or visiting the Louvre in Paris, we would rekindle our friendship and give our relationship the time it deserved. Some of the happiest moments in my life have been sitting across the table from my friends, chatting about the silliest and most random things that come to mind. Nothing can replace the deep personal connections that make us feel good about ourselves and others.

Develop a Spiritual Life

A spiritual life can take on many different meanings for different people. For some it is the same as religion; for others it has nothing to do with religion. I like to think of a spiritual life as a belief in a higher power or order of things in which the individual is only part of the whole rather than the whole itself. Spirituality is about a journey seeking wisdom, striving for personal growth, forging deep bonds with others, and searching for meaning. Leading a spiritual life is also about humility and understanding your own limitations. People who are spiritual often work hard at doing what is right and fair, and they are tolerant of differences and more willing to forgive.

Spirituality for many is a way of pursuing a meaningful life in which we use our talents to serve that larger force, whether it is a community or causes such as social justice, world hunger, a green environment, or other big-ticket issues. One definition does not fit all, nor is there a right or wrong way to

Simple Steps to Develop a Spiritual Life

Set aside at least a few quiet minutes every day to say a prayer.

Think of five ways that you can improve the conditions of those around you.

Practice finding the good in others and in difficult situations.

Love others not just in words or thoughts but through the generosity of actions.

Humbly accept and honor the concept of your relatively smaller place within a greater and bigger universe.

Spend at least an hour during the day focusing on good thoughts and positive energy.

Release anger and grudges you still have in your heart from past misdeeds.

Make a practice of doing good things for others on a regular basis.

Ask others about their struggles and triumphs. Make a real investment in the lives and well-being of those around you.

Recognize that there is a higher force in your life. While you may not be able to see, define, or touch it, recognize its presence and vast capabilities.

express spirituality. It is really all about what you think is meaningful and worthy of your service.

Forgive

When I was a little kid, one of my teachers would always say to whoever was pouting, "Smile. It's a lot less work. Frowning requires a lot more muscles than smiling." The lesson was simple even to us elementary school children: It takes a lot more effort to be sad than it does to be happy. My Sunday school teacher was famous for saying, "The more time you spend frowning, the less time you can spend smiling." By most definitions she was a very happy woman.

A similar analogy exists when it comes to forgiving or refusing to forgive. Past events that are painful, disappointing, and disturbing can scar an individual for life. Whether it is being molested as a child, having your girlfriend dump you as a teenager, or being falsely accused of something you didn't do, if the event is traumatic enough, it is unlikely you will ever be able to purge it completely from your memory. So how does one move on? That is where and why forgiveness is key.

Forgiveness is all about letting go, shedding resentments and the desire to get even with those who have wronged you. Once someone has been mistreated, the longing for revenge is extremely powerful. This longing becomes restrictive and unproductive because it keeps you bound to the offense that was committed against you rather than freeing you to move on to seize happiness in the present and future. Forgiveness is so potent that it can flip you 180 degrees. In an instant you can move from anger and vindictiveness to having compassion and feelings of understanding for the person who hurt you.

Not being able to forgive does a lot more harm than good. You are suddenly consumed by all types of negative feelings, which continue to grow the longer you hold on to the anger. When we haven't forgiven and moved on, we constantly replay the offending situation in our minds, thus crowding out more positive thoughts. There are those who hold on to grudges for years, long after the sting of their original hurt has gone away. These people are stuck; they are holding on to a bitterness simply for the sake of holding on. A tremendous amount of negative psychological and physical energy is required to remain angry or vindictive toward someone who has wronged you. But forgiving the transgressor is the fastest way to ensure that you are no longer consumed by the negative thoughts of revenge or anger.

Forgiveness might become a bigger part of our lives if we truly understood what it means and its benefits. Forgiving someone does *not* mean you condone what the person did, nor does it mean you have to forget the transgression. The act or situation that offended you will always remain a part of your life, and you will probably always remember it. Forgiveness doesn't mean you are minimizing the severity of the transgression. Forgiveness is more about the forgiver than the person being forgiven. Forgiving actually frees you from the negative mental imprisonment that entraps you when you can't let go of the past misdeed. Scientists have studied the benefits of letting go, and these include less anger, less stress, more optimism, fewer anxiety symptoms (irritability, difficulty concentrating, excessive worrying and tension, unrealistic view of problems, restlessness, or feeling edgy), lower blood pressure, lower heart rate, less depression, improved cardiovascular function, diminished chronic pain, healthier relationships, more friendships, and better reported health.[8]

While forgiveness is not always easy and often something you can't do immediately after the offending situation, it is important to identify the signs that tell you it's time to bury the hatchet. These signs include the following:

Being told you have a chip on your shoulder
Frequent feelings of being misunderstood by others
Persistent thoughts of the offending situation
Others feeling it is unpleasant to be around you
Having frequent outbursts of anger even over
the most trivial of incidents
Using alcohol, drugs, or cigarettes to
medicate your pain
Symptoms of anxiety or depression

General feelings of worthlessness or hopelessness
in other areas of your life
Being consumed by thoughts of getting revenge

For most, forgiveness is not something that happens auto-matically. Like many things in life, it's a process. An effective place to start is by taking a few minutes to weigh the benefits of forgiveness against the costs of holding on to a grudge. Next, in a calm and nonjudgmental manner as possible, review the of-fending situation. Look at it from all sides and not just yours in which you feel victimized. Was your reaction more than what the offense dictated? How has this situation and your reaction to it impacted your life? Does what happened and all its nega-tivity have the right to occupy so much of your time and men-tal space?

Putting the offending event in context with the rest of your life often reduces its importance and allows you to see how much of a waste of time it is to dwell on something that is in the past and is only standing in the way of your striving for-ward and getting on with being happy and participating in the more productive aspects of life. Define yourself not by your hurt but by how you are able to find compassion and under-standing in the face of a perceived slight. To get even more out of your forgiveness, just don't tell yourself that you're going to let go, but let the other person also know how you feel.

YOUR **HAPPY** PLAN

A. EACH WEEK PERFORM THREE HAPPINESS BOOSTERS LISTED IN THIS CHAPTER.

B. EACH WEEK READ AN ARTICLE ABOUT A PERSON, PLACE, OR THING THAT YOU DON'T ALREADY KNOW.

C. EACH MONTH ENCOURAGE SOMEONE TO DO BETTER OR FEEL BETTER OR BELIEVE IN HIMSELF OR HERSELF.

D. IDENTIFY TWO OR THREE PEOPLE WHO YOU'VE HAD AN UNPLEASANT INTERACTION WITH AND HAVE YET TO FORGIVE. CALL THEM UP OR VISIT THEM AND FORGIVE THEM IN PERSON.

10

Painting Your Life's Landscape

✧

And in the end, it's not the years in your life that count.
It's the life in your years.

—ABRAHAM LINCOLN

Most people are either afraid or too superstitious to think about their own death and what the world would look like without them. Instead, we are encouraged to remain focused on life and the opportunities it presents for us to be happy and successful. But taking a peek at the ending is not always a spoiler. It can give us a chance to shape the events and circumstances leading up to it. By considering your mortality and the fact that your life is not endless, you are better able to focus your attention and efforts on what life has to offer. So many people die without maximizing their opportunities. By that I don't mean they never get a chance to own a mansion, become president, or fly around the world on a private jet. Maximizing life means finding purpose and true meaning in what you do and pursuing activities that will not only bring you pleasure but can have long-lasting implications even after you're gone.

There is a lot to be learned about happiness by looking at the lives and mental well-being of older adults. The popular belief is that as people age they become more unhappy. Their bodies become less functional, the world begins to ignore them, and they are increasingly reminded that their time here on earth is steadily coming to an end. The caricature of a cantankerous senior citizen sitting in a nursing home complaining about the food is our stereotype of the unhappy elderly. We are conditioned to think that Grandpa will turn into a grumpy old man as he climbs into his seventies and beyond. Not so, says Susan Turk Charles, a professor at the University of California–Irvine. She looked at several studies dealing with aging and mental health, and found that in general the older people get, the happier they are.[1]

Charles says happiness and emotional well-being improve with time for several reasons. Older adults exert greater emotional control and thus are less prone to the highs and lows of younger people as they struggle to deal with various life circumstances. Older adults also learn how to avoid or limit stressful situations. Experience is one of life's best teachers, and once you have been in enough situations, you learn which mistakes not to make again and which traps to avoid. The studies also show that the senior population is less likely than younger adults to let negative comments or criticism bother them. They are much less likely to care what other people think of them.

An older person is fully aware that regardless of how great or difficult his life has been, the time he has left is growing shorter by the day. Except for those struck with depression, dementia, or other serious illnesses, the vast majority of older people want to make the best of the time that's remaining. Many things that were important to them in their thirties and forties are no longer on the priority list. They now spend a large chunk of their time taking advantage of opportunities they otherwise would have squandered or didn't have time for before.

What has taken decades for older people to figure out could have great benefit for younger people who are still finding their way in life. As we go about forging our own paths and painting our life's landscape, we would do well to adopt the lessons of our elders: maintaining an emotional balance, keeping stress to a minimum, taking personal criticism with a grain of salt, and making the most of every day. While it is important to fall every once in a while and scrape your knees, you don't have to fall to the point of breaking your bones in order to collect the valuable lessons of life. For example, those who have mismanaged their money and get their credit cards cut off have scraped their knees, but those who have lost their house and had to declare bankruptcy have broken their bones.

As I consider the wisdom that has been shared with me by older people in my life, I often think about how aging makes us humble. Young and vibrant and full of bravado and self-importance, in many of our minds we become the center of the universe. But older people have a fuller view and are quick to point out how small we really are in the grander scheme of life—even the most celebrated and famous of us.

I remember spending practically the entire day watching the funeral services of political luminaries President Ronald Reagan and Senator Ted Kennedy. I was captivated by the ceremonial pageantry as well as the precision of a day's worth of activities. It seemed as if even the smallest detail had been planned with meticulous care and timed to the second. The swarm of network cameras didn't miss one handshake between political rivals or a single tear of the grieving widow. Both funerals were similar in that throughout the news coverage the networks reviewed the deceased's long list of personal and professional accomplishments as well as their missteps. Both men lived full lives and seemed to be happy while doing so. But something else also struck me in the midst of these national days of mourning in which flags flew at half-staff and political pundits tried to one-up one another in describing the impact their deaths would have on the country: Time never stopped. The mailman delivered the mail, school buses continued to pick up and drop off children, and the streets were filled with people carrying on their daily regimens. Regardless of how wealthy, influential, or revered the person was, the clock does not stop upon their death, and other people do not stop living. Whether it is a fallen pop icon such as Michael Jackson, a superstar such as Paul Newman, or a towering political figure, the world continues to turn and life goes on.

It is important for us all to avoid exaggerating our importance or taking ourselves too seriously regardless of how successful we are or how much others admire us. Life is bigger than all of us, and it teaches us that we are only bit players on an enormous stage that affords us our moment in the spotlight but then moves on to showcase someone else the second we have made our exit. This important lesson in humility can help us take better advantage of our stage time by not sitting down and believing our own headlines but, rather, continuing to perform good deeds and maximizing the time we have at center stage.

Those who achieve happiness understand the basic fact that regardless of how much fun you're having or how many things you accomplish, life through the lens of history is incredibly short. When you take a long view, even reaching one hundred years old, which we consider a major accomplishment, it

Wisdom from Our Elders

Don't waste time worrying about things you can't control.

You can't fight every battle. Choose which ones are worth fighting and let the others go.

When deciding on a life partner, think about whether this is the person you want to grow old with, not someone who just satisfies you now.

Surround yourself with good people. Goodness is contagious.

Don't love only from your heart. Love also from your head.

Live your life to the fullest. Tomorrow isn't promised to anyone.

It takes more muscles to frown than it does to smile.

Enjoy even the smallest of life's blessings. You never know when the next one is coming.

The best way to receive is to give.

Happiness is a happy home.

barely registers on man's timeline. But we still have an opportunity nevertheless to have an impact on the world. Do we live with an understanding of our true potential?

I was in the airport the other day checking in for a flight to Los Angeles. I was happy to see Charlotte, a customer service representative whom I hadn't seen in many months. We hugged, exchanged pleasantries, and got caught up with the goings-on of our lives. What always amazes me about Charlotte is how energetic and enthusiastic she is about her job despite every day having to contend with unusual challenges, including rude passengers. Even in the most trying of circumstances she maintains her patience and cheerful attitude. The other thing about her that is amazing is her appearance. Trim and always well groomed, Charlotte looks no older than 50. Her real age is 69. I once made her show me her driver's license to prove it.

"How's life treating you?" I asked.

"No complaints," she said with a smile. "Just finishing up a busy summer."

"You look great as always," I said.

She leaned in to me across the counter and cupped her mouth. "I'll be seventy in a few months," she whispered. "Don't tell anybody."

"Seventy? Unbelievable. I just can't believe how great you look." She handed me my boarding pass. "So when are you going to retire and start enjoying life?"

"Retire?" she said, waving me off. "I'm not even thinking about retirement. What would I do?"

"Live life," I said. "Travel the world and see foreign lands. Spend more time with your family. Enjoy your hobbies. Do things that are important to you."

"Oh, I don't know," she said. "This keeps me busy, gives me something to do. I've been doing it for thirty-one years. This is all that I know."

"Thirty-one year, is a long run," I said. "But think about all the other things you could do. Pursue your passions while you're healthy and full of energy. Don't wait too long. Life can change in an instant."

Life is full of renewal and opportunities, and how we embrace them gives our existence texture. Imagine a master painting that's never finished. Each day you make a little progress, and then the next day you go back to the unfinished work and tweak it by adding and subtracting elements. But when you can only build on previous work, you become limited by what you can paint. For example, if you're in the midst of painting a forest full of tall trees and hanging vines, it is rather difficult to wake up the next day and suddenly turn that painting into the beach and ocean.

But think about how liberating it is to be able to wake up

every morning and paint whatever comes to mind, regardless of what you have previously painted. It is this new beginning that represents the opportunities of life. We have to treat each day like a blank canvas on which we can paint. Yesterday you might have been painting flowers, but today you can paint cars or horses. A new day represents a chance for renewal. What happened yesterday can't be changed, but with the rise of the sun every morning comes the opportunity to travel in a different direction and try new experiences.

Too often we carry over the baggage of yesterday into the possibilities of today and tomorrow. This produces stagnation and stifles creativity, imprisoning us in the thoughts and behaviors of the past. But those who are happy or seriously in search of happiness allow themselves the psychological freedom to get up on a new day and declare that even though yesterday was tough, today there's a chance for things to be better. Those who believe in renewal and hope are constantly reaching for that blank canvas and filling it with fresh images and interpretations, guided by unrestricted possibilities rather than what others dictate they create.

It is unreasonable to think that we can go through life ignoring anything stressful or troubling from the previous day and remember only the positive things that have happened. The trick, however, is to truly *believe* that a new day represents a new opportunity to improve on the negative and emphasize the positive. Let's say you have fallen behind on your rent payment and receive a sharply worded letter from your landlord demanding that you get caught up on what you owe or face eviction. Just by going to sleep and getting up the next morning with a positive attitude doesn't mean your problem is going to magically disappear. But your approach to the possibility of a solution can make a tremendous difference in how you handle the problem and the potential outcome. Those who are most successful in dealing with their problems improve their chances of success *first* by their attitude, and *then* by their actions. You must first have hope and the optimistic belief that something will change for the better either through your own directed actions or through circumstances that you can't control. An example of directed action might be something such as getting a temporary loan from a relative or friend to get you out of an immediate financial jam. An example of circumstantial change might be suddenly getting a promotion at work that will increase your salary and help you close the gap on the bills you owe.

Patience is another key ingredient in being able to shake off the drudgery of yesterday so that you can take advantage of a fresh start. Most problems or difficult situations are not going to simply disappear overnight. They will likely take time and your persistence in finding an effective resolution. Unless yesterday's concerns are life-threatening, however, you have to put the problem(s) in perspective and believe that regardless of how difficult the situation may be, life goes on and in some way or another things are going to be worked out. Making your troubles more than what they really are or should be will overshadow the calm and optimistic approach you need to take so that a new day truly means a new opportunity.

While we all must make our own decisions on what to paint on our canvas of life, there are five universal questions that may help you formulate your thoughts and stimulate creativity.

1. **Am I doing what matters?** Think about undertaking challenges that aren't based on what they will deliver to you right away. Try to pursue those tasks which have implications that stretch beyond you. Will others benefit from what you accomplish? Will your actions and the outcome of your actions have a broader societal or community impact? So much of what we focus our efforts on has to do with our own individual achievements. But we also must be aware of our relationship to others and the world at large and what kinds of contributions we might make to improve both.

2. **Am I chasing my dreams?** Even if your circumstances don't allow you to pursue your dreams full-time, are you doing something at least every week that puts you closer to realizing your dreams? So many people have dreams but keep them in the backseat, not giving them much attention and sometimes forgetting that they're even there.

Most of us don't have the luxury to only pursue our passions, because we have practical tasks that must be accomplished—such as paying bills and shopping for household goods. But while we give the necessary attention to what needs to be done to get through the day, we can't forget the dreams, passions, and goals that not only excite us but give meaning to our existence.

3. **Am I spending time with those I love?** Regrets about a career decision that didn't work out or the purchase of a type of car is nothing compared to the regret of not spending enough time with those you love and expressing your affection. Give the roses to people while they can smell them. The person in the casket can't see or smell the roses at his funeral. So many people end up second-guessing themselves because they start to realize too late all of the opportunities they missed to spend quality time with loved ones. Mothers often get this right. I think of the example set by a friend of mine who had worked for years for a celebrated morning show on a major network. She had made so many personal sacrifices until finally she got the big promotion to senior management. It was a job she had always wanted, and one that made her part of an elite club in the news business. But then she got pregnant and gave birth to her first daughter. She planned to take three months off and then return to work. To the surprise

of all of us who had watched her work so hard for many years to land her coveted job, she couldn't pull herself away from her baby and handed in her resignation. When I found out what she had done and asked her about it, she said, "I had to take a look at what was most important to me. I have had a good career in the news business and have done lots of great things, but I realized that at the end of the day there will always be another opportunity somewhere to produce another segment on a show, but there won't always be another opportunity to watch my daughter grow and become a little girl. I will never get that time back."

4. **Am I doing something that will help others?** Studies have clearly shown that committing acts of kindness increases happiness. Helping others doesn't always mean writing a check. Acts of goodwill such as reading to children at your local library or delivering meals to the elderly and sick can go a lot further than giving money. Many of us are preoccupied with self-preservation, doing those things that we need to do to survive or get ahead. Whether it is angling for a job promotion, tending to the needs of our family, or spending our free time pursuing hobbies, it is so easy to be consumed with activities that deal only with our personal achievements. By the time we complete all of the things we need to do during the course of the day, the last thing on our mind is adding more to our

schedule. So while the idea of helping others is appealing, we often don't act on it because our time is limited.

5. **Do I feel good going to sleep at night?** Having a reliable moral compass and using it can do a lot to ease one's mind. Most of us know the right thing to do, but often take the easy way out. Guilt is a powerful emotion, one that can weigh on your mind with crushing pressure. Look at some of the coldest criminals who have stumped investigators. Some have been so good that they seemed to have gotten away with the perfect crime, not leaving enough clues for investigators to make any progress in identifying them. But there has been many a time when an investigation has stalled and the detectives were not sure where to turn next and the case has gone cold. Then suddenly, for no apparent reason, the person who committed the crime just walks through the door and turns himself in, saying he could no longer live with the guilt controlling his every thought, even though he may have never been discovered. That is how powerful the feelings of guilt can be. When faced with right or wrong, good or bad, think about which decision will allow you to feel good about yourself as your head hits the pillow that night.

There is a beginning and an end to life. But what comes in between is what's most important. It is through good deeds, selflessness, great artistic expression, pioneering legislation, and many other actions that we continue our spiritual existence on earth while our physical presence has moved on. It is about legacy—what we leave behind to be admired by and enjoyed by future generations. It doesn't mean you have to discover the next great vaccine or win a landmark case in front of the U.S. Supreme Court. What it means is that in your own way you leave footprints—evidence years from now that you were here and contributed to the greater good, maximizing life's opportunities rather than squandering them by living only for yourself and the moment. Those who recognize this too late find themselves drowning in a sea of regrets.

I remember as a young boy sitting with a group of older teenagers on a lazy summer afternoon. We had just finished playing a game of basketball and were strewn about the park grass, trying to cool down in the shade. Fatigued and in no hurry to go anywhere, this group of guys started talking about what they wanted to do with their lives and how determined they were not to let opportunities pass. We loved our hometown and small community, but we had dreams of venturing out into the big world, exploring faraway lands, and meeting new people who talked different languages and followed different social customs. Then one of the older guys claimed that he always used the "rocking chair test." Confused, the others asked him to explain.

"It's like this, guys," he began. "You have to accept the fact that all of us will one day be old. We're not going to be able to play basketball or chase girls or any of that stuff for the rest of our lives. One day we're gonna find ourselves sitting on a porch in a rocking chair and thinking about our lives and all the memories from when we were young. I don't wanna be in that rocking chair thinking about all the things I could've and should've done but didn't when I had the chance. Regrets. I'm not going to have any regrets."

As I got older, I found myself using that rocking chair test with increasing frequency. Should I go on this trip to Brazil with my college friends even though I'm short on funds and the money could be more prudently spent on my increasing stack of high-interest credit card bills? I did the rocking chair test and went to Brazil. I was offered a chance to report for a television station although it meant consuming what little free time I had and making my medical residency training, which was already difficult, practically impossible. I did the rocking chair test and became a medical journalist while at the same time finishing my training. After completing my medical training and finally taking back my life, I was asked to join the board of a nonprofit that gave underprivileged children an after-school facility where they could participate in sports, the arts, and tutoring. While a noble cause, this would require time and energy, two things I had just regained in my life. I had been looking forward to catching up on things I had missed the last several years, such as all-night parties in downtown New York City, vacations to

The Rocking Chair Test

Every decision, regardless of how small it is, has consequences. It often helps to take some time to think about the decision, not only in the context of the present but its impact on your future. Ask yourself these simple questions first and remember that even if you make a bad decision, there's something you can learn from it that can be beneficial in the future:

What are the short-term and long-term consequences of the decision you're about to make?

Does this decision feel right and align with your moral compass?

If you were observing someone else in a similar situation making the decision you're about to make, would you approve?

When you look back and evaluate this decision, will it be one you remember favorably?

Will this decision set off a cascade of events that has undesirable consequences?

Look in the Rearview Mirror

In this exercise, push the fast-forward button. You are now eighty years old and sitting quietly on a park bench watching ducks glide by in a small pond. The sun is shining through the foliage as the birds fly from tree to tree. You are at peace. You feel complete. You start thinking about how you've arrived at where you are in life. Take a look back at five major life categories. Imagine the experiences, feelings, and personal development that occurred through the years. Is what you are seeing what you wanted to happen?

1. **Family.** If you had children and a spouse or significant other, imagine what the parenting and shared family journey looked like. Think about the significant milestones: school graduations, entrances into college, your child's wedding, family vacations, family holidays, the birth of grandchildren, etc.

2. **Career.** What was your career trajectory like? Did you stay at one job or switch careers? Were you happy in your chosen career? Did you feel fulfilled?

3. **Leisure.** Did you have fun? What other states and countries did you visit? Did you fully enjoy the birthday parties, holiday parties, and social gatherings? Did you pursue a hobby? What kind of people did you meet? What kind of friends did you make? What sorts of art and entertainment did you enjoy? What excitement did you find falling in love?

4. **Humanitarianism.** Did you give to others? Were you selfless or selfish? Did you make life better for others? Did you meaningfully engage in helping others pursue their dreams?

5. **Physical World.** What kinds of houses did you live in? Was there a favorite room you enjoyed most—maybe the sunroom overlooking the garden or a room with a great view of the skyline? Was there a hike, a lake, or a place in nature that meant something to you? Did you own a sanctuary, a place where you could escape the busyness of life and enjoy the company of family and friends or even alone time? What did you look like when you got dressed up—the clothes, shoes, and jewelry?

tropical resorts, and golfing. But I did the rocking chair test and joined the nonprofit board.

By *imagining* what you might see in the rearview mirror you have a chance to avoid making the wrong turn, blowing through that stop sign, or getting pulled over in a speed trap. Looking in the rearview mirror can help guide your hand as you paint that landscape of life. When it comes to the fullness of life, one doesn't measure it by the quantity of experiences but by their diversity and quality.

Find new challenges and discover new things to bolster your happiness. None of us is dealt the same hand in life. The child of wealthy parents who spends most of his formative years in boarding school might have everything one can imagine from a material standpoint but still be deprived of a deep and meaningful relationship with his parents and the love that comes with that. A young girl whose family is suffering from financial hardship might not be able to afford private tutors and preparatory classes, but she is able to learn invaluable lessons about life by watching her parents work, struggle, and make sacrifices so that she might have the best education possible. Whatever our advantages or disadvantages, positions or dispositions, we must take our circumstances and focus on the positive rather than the negative. Happiness is there for *all* of us, and it doesn't ask us about our social standing, level of education, or the designer labels in our clothes.

In my travels I meet people who are down on their luck or

have encountered a rough patch on their journey. I tell them that they *must* believe in their capacity for greatness, but in doing so they must avoid making comparisons. Trying to match or exceed the accomplishments of others is a useless exercise that can often lead to discouragement and a false sense of failure. If you are a cable installer, be the best cable installer you can be. If you are an investment banker, do your job to the best of your ability. While society has unfortunately fabricated a tier system of worthiness when it comes to things such as employment, education, and financial status, it is your responsibility to completely ignore this meaningless hierarchy. Instead, stay focused on challenging and pushing yourself to new heights and accomplishments.

Happiness is not about how many toys you've collected at the end of the day but how many toys you've helped give away to others.

A. CREATE A SENTENCE THAT DESCRIBES HOW YOU WANT PEOPLE TO

REMEMBER YOU, AND MODIFY THIS SENTENCE PERIODICALLY IF
YOU DESIRE.

....

....

**B. NAME THE FIVE THINGS YOU HOPE TO HAVE ACCOMPLISHED BY
THE END OF YOUR LIFE.**

....

....

....

....

....

**C. WRITE A BRIEF DESCRIPTION OF WHAT YOU THINK YOUR LEGACY
WILL BE.**

....

....

....

....

....

notes

INTRODUCTION: THE EPIPHANY

1. Seligman, M.E.P., and Csikszentmihalyi, M. (2000). Positive psychology: An introduction. *American Psychologist* 55, 5–14.
2. Seligman, M.E.P., and Csikszentmihalyi, M. (2000). Positive psychology: An introduction. *American Psychologist* 55, 5–14.

I: WHAT IS HAPPINESS?

1. Harper, Matthew. (August 21, 2004). *Money Won't Buy You Happiness.* Forbes.com.
2. Include Tunney citation information
3. Interview with John Templeton Foundation.
4. Ben-Shahar, Tal. *The Question of Happiness.* Writers Club Press (August 2002).
5. Lykken, D. T. and Tellegen, A. (1996). Happiness is a stochastic phenomenon. *Psychological Science* 7, 186–89.
6. Lyubomirsky, S.; Sheldon, K. M.; and Schkade, D. (2005). Pursuing happiness: The architecture of sustainable change. *Review of General Psychology 9,* 111–31.
7. White, A. (2007). A global projection of subjective well-being: A challenge to positive psychology? *Psychtalk* 56, 17–20.
8. Carroll, J. (August 24, 2007). Worker's Average Commute Round-Trip Is 46 Minutes in a Typical Day. Gallup News Service.
9. Saad, L. (August 21, 2008). U.S. Workers' Job Satisfaction Is Relatively High. Gallup News Service.

NOTES

10. Carroll, J. (December 31, 2007). Most Americans "Very Satisfied" with Their Personal Lives. Gallup News Survey.
11. Diener, E.; Emmons, R.A.; Larsen, R.J.; and Griffin, S. (1985). The satisfaction with life scale. *Journal of Personality Assessment* 49, 71–75.

2: PLAY TO YOUR STRENGTHS

1. Seligman, M.E.P.; Steen, T.; Park, N.; and Peterson, C. (2005). Positive psychology progress: Empirical validation of interventions. *American Psychologist 60(5)*, 410–21.

3: THE SILVER LINING

1. Maruta, T., et al., Optimists vs. pessimists: Survival rate among medical patients over a 30-year period. *Mayo Clinic Proceedings* (2000). 75(2): 140–43.
2. Giltay, E.J.; Geleijnse, J. M.; Zitman, F. G.; Hoekstra, T.; and Schouten, E. G. (2004). Dispositional optimism and all-cause and cardiovascular mortality in a prospective cohort of elderly dutch men and women. *Archives of General Psychiatry.* 61: 1126–35.
3. Seligman, M.E.P.; Nolen-Hoeksema, S.; Thornton, N.; and Thornton, K.M. (1990). Explanatory style as a mechanism of disappointing athletic performance. *Psychological Science* 1, 143–46.
4. Sharot, T.; Riccardi, A.M.; Raio, C.M.; and Phelps, E.A. (2007). Neural mechanisms mediating optimism bias. *Nature* 450: 102–106.

5: NORTH OF ZERO

1. Diener, E., and Seligman, M.E.P. (2002). Very happy people. *Psychological Science* 13(1), 81–84.
2. Kahneman, D.; Krueger, A. B.; Schkade, D. A.; Schwarz, N.; and Stone, A. A. (2004). A survey method for characterizing daily life experience: The day reconstruction method. *Science* 306, 1776–80.
3. Lyubomirsky, S. *The How of Happiness: A Scientific Approach to Getting the Life You Want.* New York: Penguin Press, 2008.
4. Fowler J. H, and Christakis, N. A. (2008) *The dynamic spread of happiness in a large social network. British Med J 337:a 2338.*
5. Shenk, J. W. "What Makes Us Happy." *The Atlantic*, June 2009.

NOTES

7: HAPPY AT WORK

1. Saad, L. (August 21, 2008). U.S. Workers' Job Satisfaction Is Relatively High. Gallup News Service.
2. Helliwell, J. F., *Well Being and Trust in the Workplace*. National Bureau of Economic Research Working Paper Series (May 2007).

8: LET IT FLOW

1. Csikszentmihalyi, M. *Finding Flow*. Basic Books, 1997.

9: HAPPINESS BOOSTERS

1. Lyubomirsky, S.; Sheldon, K. M.; and Schkade, D. (2005). Pursuing happiness: The architecture of sustainable change. *Review of General Psychology 9*, 111–31.
2. Boehm, J. K.; and Lyubomirsky, S. (in press). The promise of sustainable happiness. In S.J. Lopez (ed.), Handbook of positive psychology (2nd ed.). Oxford University Press.
3. Emmons, R. A. *Thanks! How the New Science of Gratitude Can Make You Happier*. Houghton Mifflin Harcourt, 2007.
4. Seligman, M.E.P.; Steen, T.; Park, N.; and Peterson, C. (2005). Positive psychology progress: Empirical validation of interventions. *American Psychologist 60(5)*, 410–21
5. Seligman, M.E.P.; Steen, T.; Park, N.; and Peterson, C. (2005). Positive psychology progress: Empirical validation of interventions. *American Psychologist 60(5)*, 410–21.
6. Dunn, E. W.; Aknin, L. B.; and Norton, M. I. (2008). Spending money on others promotes happiness. *Science*. 319:1687–88.
7. Diener, E., and Seligman, M.E.P. (2002). Very happy people. *Psychological Science 13*, 80–83.
8. Seligman, M.E.P. *Authentic Happiness*. New York: Free Press (2002), and Healy, M. "Forgive and be well?" *Los Angeles Times* (December 31, 2007).

10: PAINTING YOUR LIFE'S LANDSCAPE

1. *Health Day News* (August 13, 2009). Good news for elderly: Happiness keeps growing.

acknowledgments

The process of writing this book is only part of the total package. There's so much else that goes into the finished product that you see on the shelf. To that end, I'd like to thank those who work tirelessly and with no public recognition to help deliver my vision to you: my crew at St. Martin's Press, including editor supreme, Elizabeth Beier, and her right hand woman, Michelle Richter, who, as always, find a way to make my ideas sing from the pages; fellow golfing zealot Steve Cohen; indefatigable leaders of the gang, Matthew Shear and Sally Richardson; PR maestros John Murphy and John Karle; promotional engines Matt Baldacci and Lisa Senz; and Rob Grom for an awesome book jacket. A tremendous personal thanks to my unrivaled family (Tristé, Dash, Declan, Ma, and Dana), who endured my periods of hibernation and annoying writing idiosyncrasies when I was "in the zone"; and my stabilizing personal assistant, Liza Rodriguez. My thanks to all of the readers out there who inspired me to write about a topic that is so deep in my heart and central to my core. I am only one of a great team and that makes me infinitely HAPPY.

index

INDEX

INDEX

INDEX

INDEX